Would You Believe It?

Would You Believe it?

Mysterious Tales From People You'd Least Expect

Selected and Edited by

Karen Stollznow

Cover art by Matthew Baxter.

"The most beautiful thing we can experience is the mysterious. It is the source of all true art and science."

Albert Einstein, *Living Philosophies.*

Contents

Acknowledgements

My sincere thanks to the authors for contributing their fascinating personal stories.

Thank you to James Alcock, Banachek, Matthew Baxter, Hal Bidlack, Matt Bille, Susan Blackmore, S.G. Browne, Brian Brushwood, Steve Cuno, S. Von Cyburg, Harry Edwards, Ken Feder, David Fitzgerald, Chris French, Sheldon Helms, Bruce Hood, George Hrab, Deborah Hyde, Ray Hyman, Lynne Kelly, Greg Laden, Dean Learner, Mike McRae, Joe Nickell, Massimo Polidoro, Donald Prothero, James Randi, Brian Regal, Eugenie Scott, Brian Sharpless, Robert Sheaffer, Aiden Sinclair, Alison Smith, Blake Smith, Hayley Stevens, James Underdown, Jeff Wagg, David Waldron, and an Anonymous author.

A special thank you goes to Matthew Baxter, Steve Cuno and Rick Duffy for their advice and additional assistance with editing and proofreading.

Hidden Truths

Forward:
James Randi

My paternal grandfather George took great joy in telling a childhood story that became his way of reminding me that truth can hide in very strange places, even in what seems to be a child's tall tale.

When he was a young boy, his family moved from Austria to Copenhagen, Denmark. At the end of their street was a big iron gate that led out to the palace grounds of the King of Denmark. Every morning on his way to school, little George passed by this gate and delivered lunch to his father, who was working at the nearby shipyards. This was the usual routine five days a week.

During that time, George was learning the new language, and having some difficulty making friends. Kids can be pretty mean at that age, in any language. And my grandfather was only child who often felt lonely. However, he did make a very unlikely friend while out exploring his new country.

Each evening when the family sat down for dinner, George delighted in telling his parents about his day. His stories began to revolve around a mysterious character he called "Mr. Christian." I imagine this was not an unusual name at that time in Denmark. But George described Mr. Christian as a large man with a big black beard who rode a big black horse and was surrounded by men with swords and giant dogs.

George's parents believed this was an imaginary friend their little son had dreamed up out of loneliness. And as time went by, Mr. Christian figured into the evening's conversation more often. One way or another, George would mention him.

"It was raining today. Mr. Christian, his giant dogs, and the men with the swords were very wet," George would say, with the wide-eyed expression that you would expect from a child speaking from imagination.

Then one day, Mr. Christian stepped over the line. He told George about some changes that were going to be taking place at the shipyards where George's father worked. Mr. Christian suggested that George's father might wish to apply for a transfer. When George presented this news at the dinner table that night his father became angry. He wasn't going to take career advice from his son's imaginary friend! And he had had enough of these tall tales about "Mr. Christian." He sat George down, looked him straight in the eye and had a serious chat with him.

"I won't have any more stories about this ghost companion of yours," he demanded. "We don't talk about this 'Mr. Christian' anymore!"

Little George became quite upset and insisted, "But... Mr. Christian is real!"

"No!" replied his father sternly. "Mr. Christian is in your head. He is an imaginary character and I don't want to hear any more about him!"

In those days, I would wager, children obeyed their fathers better than they do today. George no longer spoke of Mr. Christian. That was the end of it. At least, for a while.

Then one evening after dinner, George's father sat down and picked up the newspaper to read the daily news. He spread wide the pages and the little boy found himself staring at a drawing of a large man with a big black beard sitting astride a big black horse, surrounded by men with swords and giant dogs.

George pointed to the picture and said to his father excitedly, "*That's* Mr. Christian!"

His father looked at the front page of the newspaper. He gazed at the image silently for a few moments before explaining calmly to his son that this was not an imaginary person, this was an illustration of King Christian IX of Denmark.

He looked back at little George's earnest face. Suddenly, it dawned on him.

"I suppose Mr. Christian *wasn't* an imaginary friend after all!" he said in surprise.

George had been talking to none other than the King of Denmark.

Every morning, "Mr. Christian" did his daily rounds of the palace grounds, taking the time to talk to his citizens. One of them was little George, on his way to deliver lunch to his father before going to school.

George had been telling the truth all along.

King Christian IX of Denmark
(Image: Wikipedia)

My grandfather never tired of telling this story because it was a great victory for him. From then on, he and his father developed a closer relationship and a better understanding of each other.

Throughout my career I have always tried to be skeptical, but I have very studiously stayed away from being cynical. As the creator of the Million Dollar Paranormal Challenge, which is an offer to pay out one million US dollars to anyone who can prove, under scientific conditions, that they have a paranormal ability, I have heard a lot of unbelievable stories over the years. However, my grandfather's story taught me that one should always listen to these first before simply dismissing them because there may be some truth hidden somewhere.

There are lessons in my grandfather's story for all of us. We should try to listen to other people, try to understand where they're coming from, and try to keep an open mind. When someone comes to us and says they have experienced something mysterious we shouldn't dismiss their claim out of hand. That isn't good skepticism. As part of the Million Dollar Paranormal Challenge we listened to the claimant's story and then investigated it further to see if there was any truth to it.

To many people, skepticism and cynicism are the same thing. But there is a great deal of difference between the two. Skepticism itself is a very healthy attitude, but that doesn't mean you should be hyper-skeptical of everything. That borders on cynicism, and that is a trap.

And if we are cynical about people's stories from the outset, we will never get to be surprised by the hidden truths that may await us.

James Randi has an international reputation as a magician and escape artist, but today he is best known as the world's most tireless investigator and demystifier of paranormal and pseudoscientific claims. He is the author of numerous books, including *The Truth About Uri Geller; The Faith Healers; Flim-Flam!*, and *An Encyclopedia of Claims, Frauds, and Hoaxes of the Occult and Supernatural*. His lectures and television appearances have delighted—and vexed—audiences around the world. web.randi.org

An Angel Visitation And A Ghostly Party

Introduction:
Karen Stollznow

I am often asked, "Have you ever had anything paranormal happen to you?" As an investigator of paranormal phenomena, I seem to surprise and disappoint the inquirer when I answer with a swift "No."

After fielding this same question many times over I started to wonder, in all of my years of pursuing the paranormal, why is it that I have never had a paranormal experience? How could I spend so many nights investigating "haunted" houses but never see a ghost? How could I trek through dense forests known for Bigfoot sightings but not come face-to-face with the hairy cryptid myself? How could I visit a UFO hotspot but not spot a UFO?

Skeptics will argue that this is because these things don't exist.

Believers might argue that skeptics never see ghosts, Bigfoot, or UFOs because the skeptics are too closed-minded. They don't attract paranormal activity because they give off negative energy. Skeptics are curmudgeons and naysayers and party poopers and debunkers and Debbie Downers. Skeptics are cynics.

I used to think, "Nothing strange has ever happened to me. I have *never* had a paranormal experience." But what exactly is a "paranormal experience" anyway? Could the paranormal be different things to different people? Could I have already experienced something that some people might understand as "paranormal"? Was I being closed-minded? Was I being a cynic? I reflected heavily on my past and remembered that I *had* experienced some weird incidents after all…

There was the time that I was walking alone at night through Gore Hill Cemetery in Sydney. The place is rumored to be haunted. And with a creepy name like that, why wouldn't it be? The cemetery opened in the mid-nineteenth century, which is old by Australian standards. One of the largest metropolitan cemeteries in the country, it has interred over 14,000 people, with the last burial taking place in 1974. Freeways and high rises have since sprung up around the cemetery, as well as a hospital. The cemetery must be a morbid sight for the patients looking out of their windows, or perhaps seen as a bad omen.

I had visited a friend who had just undergone emergency surgery in that hospital. He was stable but being watched closely by his doctors. After my visit, I decided to take a walk through Gore Hill instead of taking the path by the main road back to my car. The cemetery was beautiful and filled with ornate crypts and statues, but the grounds weren't well maintained, and climbing roses, wisteria and weeds grew with wild abandon. During the day you could see a rust-colored fungus growing on the tombstones that looked like blood.

Gore Hill Cemetery
(Photo: The Daily Telegraph)

After years of neglect, the brick paths were uneven, and I tripped on a tree root and fell. When I got back on my feet I looked up into the dark night sky. Suddenly, I saw a glowing white angel above me. She hovered over a tombstone, looked straight at me, and pointed a finger menacingly towards the stars. I was startled to say the least. Was this a sign that my sick friend was going to die? Or was this a warning that something terrible was about to happen to me? My night vision has never been very good so I blinked, rubbed my eyes and looked again, but this time I only saw the shadowy outline of a statue. It was just a white marble sculpture of an angel that had been lit up by a bright streetlight in the background. However, the angel wasn't looking at me, she was looking downwards, and she didn't have a finger pointed towards the sky, her hands were clasped in prayer.

I was a little shaken at the time, but I eventually explained the sight as an optical illusion. Nothing bad happened to me, at least not at that time, and my friend recovered quickly from his surgery.

I soon forgot about the incident.

Several years later, I was visiting the North Head Quarantine Station in Manly, which was built on a headland overlooking Sydney Harbour. From 1828 until 1972 (yes, this is another old place by Australian standards), "The Station" was established to isolate passengers from migrant ships that were suspected to be carrying contagious diseases, such as Spanish influenza, cholera, smallpox, and bubonic plague. Quarantining was enforced in the hope that these diseases would be contained and wouldn't spread to the general population.

If an infection broke out on board during a voyage, the captain raised a yellow flag and moored at the Station. When the passengers disembarked, healthy people were placed into class-segregated areas that reflected their fare (because the shipping companies paid for their accommodation.) Sick people were taken straight to the hospital to be nursed back to health. Hopefully. These immigrants had dreams of starting a new life in a new country, but many who entered the grounds never left. (The headland used to be dotted with headstones, until it was realized that this gloomy view was bad for the morale of the arriving passengers.) Some people believe that the spirits of those who died at the Quarantine Station are still there. It is said to be Australia's most haunted place.

North Head Quarantine Station
(Photo: The Oz Effect)

My friends and I were on a ghost tour of the site, but it wasn't our first. Over the years, we had done that tour so many times that we knew more ghost stories than the tour guides. On previous visits we'd found inscriptions on the rocks carved by those who'd been quarantined and we had also discovered headstones in the bushes, but we'd never seen or heard anything strange, until that night.

Most of the original buildings still stand on the site, including the hospital and the morgue. We were outside the first class quarters when we all heard a party being held in one of the rooms. We heard tinkling piano music, a woman's laughter, and the sounds of champagne glasses clinking together in a toast. We assumed that the room must have been rented out for a special function. Curious, we pushed open the heavy doors, only to discover that there was no party. The lights were off and the room was completely empty.

We looked at each other in surprise. Then we searched the area, although we couldn't find a celebration being held anywhere on the grounds. What had we just heard? The building had once contained a smoking room for the men and a sitting room for the ladies. Had we just heard the sounds of a phantom party from a bygone era?

Later that night we heard more eerie music and voices, so we explained the ghostly noises as probably being the sounds of a real party that streamed in from the mainland.

Again, I soon forgot about the incident.

I filed away these events in my memory because I had made sense of them. To me, they no longer stood out as mysterious. Certainly, they were mysterious experiences that could be categorized as paranormal-like, but I had categorized them differently. I had arrived at reasonable explanations and then forgotten about them, but this isn't how everyone else might see them. I accepted my experience in the cemetery as an optical illusion although it might be explained as an angel visitation by another person. The fragmented sounds of a party that I believed to be streaming in from the mainland might be perceived as a ghostly party by someone else. People make sense of their personal experiences in different ways and it's easy to understand why some might interpret these strange experiences as paranormal.

Paranormal experiences are all in the interpretation.

To this day, I still believe in those natural explanations, but I can't recreate the experiences exactly so I'll never know if I am right or wrong. But does it matter anyway? Everyone loves a good ghost story. Perhaps I am just spoiling the fun? So, when people ask, "Have you ever had anything paranormal happen to you?" I now answer, "Well, there was this one time..." and I talk about my mysterious experiences, along with my theories of what might have really happened. I share a few of these stories in my chapter of this book.

When I tell my stories to other skeptics I've found that I'm not alone. Many science-minded people have had strange personal experiences that have given them pause. For example, in *The Skeptic* (Australia, 1991, Volume 11, No.3, p.21), author Harry Edwards wrote about a bizarre coincidence that happened to him during a trip to the Mayan city of Chichen Itza.

"I joined the bus queue to return to my hotel. In front of me was a stranger with an Australian flag on his backpack.
"Hi, where are you from?" I asked.
"Sydney," he replied.
"No big deal," I thought, "the odds are about one in five."
"What suburb?"
"Newport," he said.

"Hey, that's a coincidence. So am I. Whereabouts?"

"Nullaburra Road."

"Amazing! I live in Nullaburra Road too. What number?"

"Three," he replied. "It's a block of home units. Do you know it?"

"Know it?" I exclaimed, "I own it..."

No doubt the more enquiring mind will wonder why I didn't know the fellow if he lived in the same building and was my tenant. The answer is that he moved in with a friend a couple of days after I left Australia for Mexico."

In *SuperSense*, psychologist Bruce Hood also recounts a peculiar coincidence.

"Weird stuff happens all the time. Some years ago, before we were married, Kim and I traveled to London. It was our first trip to the capital, and we decided to use the Underground. London's Underground train system transports more than three million passengers every single day, and so we were relieved to find two seats together inside one of the crowded carriages. As we settled down, I looked up to read the various advertisements, as one does to avoid direct eye contact with fellow passengers, but then I noted that the young man seated opposite seemed vaguely familiar. I nudged Kim and said that the man looked remarkably like her brother, whom we last heard was traveling in South America. It had been years since we last saw him. Kim stared at the man, and at that instant the man looked up from the paper he was reading and returned the stare. For what seemed a very long time, the two held each other's gaze before the quizzical expression on the man's face turned to a smile and he said, "Kim?" Brother and sister could not believe their chance encounter."

It appeared to me as though it was not the exception but the norm for people to have paranormal-like experiences. The commonness of these strange incidents explains why a belief in the paranormal is so widespread. Dr. James Alcock writes about this in his afterword. He explains that, given the way our brains work, sooner or later most of us are going to have what seem to be paranormal experiences. And if we haven't had one, we probably know of someone who has. Having a paranormal-like experience is a human experience.

So, we can put to rest the notion that skeptics never have anything paranormal happen to them because they are closed-minded cynics, or they give off negative energy. These are just stereotypes, for the most part. Weird things happen to us all, it's just a matter of how we frame our experiences. A chance happening might be seen as synchronicity or a coincidence. A crop circle might be seen as a message from an alien spacecraft or a prank. Some look for supernatural explanations while others seek natural explanations.

In this book, a number of prominent scientists, skeptics, humanists, magicians and authors share their strangest, spookiest experiences, in their own words. World-famous mentalist Banachek, skeptical paranormal investigator Joe Nickell, psychologist Susan Blackmore, and musician George Hrab are among those you'd least expect to tell mysterious tales.

This collection includes stories about a wide range of paranormal phenomena, including ghost and UFO sightings, a Bigfoot encounter, séances, superstitions, strange animals, demonic possession, out-of-body-experiences, past lives, episodes of missing time, and one case where time stood still. You will read about a poltergeist in a bakery, a genius baby, a haunted concert hall, stone carvings that vanish and reappear mysteriously, a one-time palm reader, intuition that led to a man finding out he had a daughter he never knew about, and a former Mormon missionary who once believed he healed a woman of a brain tumor.

These experiences seemed paranormal at first. Sometimes the authors have explanations for their weird experiences. Sometimes they don't. Some of these stories leave a question mark–but it's okay to admit, "I don't know." Of course, just because something is unexplained doesn't mean it is inexplicable. You might have fun trying to draw your own conclusions about these mysterious experiences. They might also remind you of your own.

Whether you believe or not, sit back and enjoy reading this collection of mysterious tales from people you'd least expect...

The (After) Life Of the Party

Matthew Baxter

It was a dark and stormy night... No, seriously. It was one of the worst blizzards that Evergreen, Colorado, had seen in years. But it never failed: If we had an overnight gig in some remote mountain town, you could bet that a near record-breaking blizzard would be joining our investigation.

Now, when I say "investigation," I'm referring to paranormal investigation. My partner Bryan Bonner and I are from Rocky Mountain Paranormal Research Society. Sure, we have the word "paranormal" in our name, but that doesn't mean we're one of those ghost-hunting groups out just to scare themselves by creeping around in cemeteries in the dead of night. Our goal is to investigate, and we actually adhere to the scientific method as closely as we can, instead of using the reality TV method.

We were at the Brook Forest Inn; a beautiful bed and breakfast nestled in the Rocky Mountains. The Swiss Chalet building was part of a Swiss-style village built back in the early 1900s. We had formed a good working relationship with the owners of the Inn and we were the only paranormal investigation team that they trusted. Many other paranormal groups have a reputation for vandalism and disrespect, but we work hard to establish ourselves as respectful and educated. If other groups wanted to investigate the Inn, the Brook Forest required them to take a class from us first. Many groups were scrambling to get into the place.

The Brook Forest Inn has a reputation for being very haunted. Edwin Jr., the original owner's son, died of pneumonia at the age of five. It is said that the ghost of the little boy can be heard laughing and running down the hallways, and he can be seen playing with a red ball. In another story, Jessica the chambermaid was murdered by her lover Carl the stable hand, who strangled her to death in room 27.

Occasionally, people who sleep in that room report waking up in the middle of the night and feeling a pair of ice-cold hands wrapped around their neck.

One ghost-hunting group believed they'd found proof of the paranormal. They supplied us with a dark, blurry photograph of a "ghost" they'd captured. We lightened up the image but still couldn't tell what it was. We asked to see the photographs taken immediately before and afterwards, but the team had deleted those because they weren't interesting. After a lot of investigation we finally identified the mysterious object. In the hotel's lobby there is a photograph of a marble statue of a lion hanging on the wall. Investigating the lobby in the dark, the ghost hunting team had snapped a photograph of a photograph...

Over the years, we have gotten to the bottom of quite a few legends associated with the Inn. There was a rumor that the original owner had built the place to be a prisoner camp run by the Nazis during World War II. It is said that there is a large amount of Nazi gold buried beneath the building, just waiting to be discovered. Some believe that Adolf Hitler himself stayed on the property. We investigated the claims and instead of discovering hidden gold, we discovered tiles on the floor in a closet that were hand-painted with a symbol that looked like a swastika. However, it wasn't a Nazi swastika, but a Native American motif known as the "Whirling Log." We eventually traced the legend to a psychic who spotted the symbol and invented the tale of Nazis and buried treasure.

There are many more ghost stories surrounding the Brook Forest Inn, but there is one that we haven't solved. This was a mysterious experience that happened to us. So, let's get back to the aforementioned dark and stormy night.

It was about 8:30 p.m. on a Friday night. As we drove up to the Inn the snow was already beginning to pile up. We trudged to the door with armloads of heavy surveillance equipment, including Electromagnetic Field (EMF) detectors and various other gauges and gadgets. Note: we don't use these devices in the same way that ghost-hunting groups do. We aren't looking for ghosts; we're searching for the truth behind the claims. You'd be surprised how often an EMF detector can offer a reasonable solution to an allegedly ghostly problem. In this very location, guests reported hearing a loud knocking sound. A ghost-hunting group spent their investigation here establishing a code so they could communicate with the "entity." (One knock for "Yes," two knocks for "No.") We instead used our EMF detectors for the purposes for which they were designed. (Hint: Not for ghost hunting.) We discovered that the mundane source of the sound was the furnace.

When we arrived, Joe, the Brook Forest Inn's caretaker, answered the front door. He knew us well from previous visits. During the winter, the place sat empty for months at a time so we could visit and test out new investigative approaches undisturbed.

"Perfect timing!" he beamed.

Joe's position as caretaker meant he was stuck alone in the old building for much of the off-season. His lonely situation was very much like that of Jack Torrance in horror writer Stephen King's book *The Shining*. Our arrival presented him with the opportunity to get out and socialize for a while.

"I'm off to the bar!" He said as he tossed us the keys and pushed his way out the door. "I'll be back when I'm back!"

Bryan and I glanced sideways at each other, shrugged and continued lugging our gear into the Inn. It has always fascinated us that paranormal investigators are entrusted with so much responsibility. Ghost hunters are not professionals that have had to complete years of schooling and rigorous training. But they boast their self-given titles anyway as they are welcomed into people's homes and businesses. Bryan and I have been given the keys to county court houses and left completely unsupervised for entire weekends, allowed entry to restricted areas on protected federal territory, and expected to somehow authorize access for federal government personnel to inspect private property.

We unpacked our equipment, decided where to set up our headquarters, and began assembling our mobile surveillance system. From start to finish it takes us about two hours to set up everything and run baseline readings on temperature and electromagnetic frequency levels. After setting up our equipment, if a mouse moves, we'll know it.

The Brook Forest Inn
(Photo: Matthew Baxter)

Another difference between ghost-hunting groups and us is that we don't assume that a location is haunted. We don't walk around asking questions of the "spirits" or try to provoke "ghosts" into materializing. Trying to interact with something that has never been proven to exist in the first place contaminates the evidence. Groups that don't practice silence as an investigation technique tend to talk all the time. Weeks later, when they are listening to their recordings, they freak out over the "ghostly" voices they hear during playback. (That wasn't a ghost. It was your *voice*, dumbass.) Instead, we sit down, shut up, and observe. We document the location, climate, and environment. If we can test a specific claim, we do that too. For example, if a resident reports that a ghostly cowboy drifts across the kitchen every day, we attempt to recreate the event to determine if there is a simple, natural explanation.

After hours of monitoring our equipment in silence, we decided to raid the kitchen for snacks. There were five of us on the team that night and our supply of M&M's was running low. To avoid recording ourselves and to save hard drive space, we paused the recording so we could "investigate" the contents of the kitchen. At that very moment, we heard the front doors downstairs swing open wide, as if a parade of people were trudging into the Inn and stomping the snow off their shoes. The jovial din of people talking and laughing filled the air. Bryan and I looked at each other in annoyance.

"Great. He's brought the bar home with him," Bryan groaned with a shake of his head.

We heard what seemed to be at least 20 people downstairs. The sound of clinking glasses suggested that the bar was now open for business too. We were very irritated by this turn of events.

"How the hell are we going to do an investigation now?" I growled.

"We can't," replied Bryan. "At least not until we kick them out of here."

Joe knew that we needed silence to conduct our investigation. He must have been very drunk to forget that fact. Reluctantly leaving the other team members with the remaining M&M's, Bryan and I headed downstairs to find Joe among the crowd of people he'd brought home with him. As we approached the stairs, the party was getting louder. As the volume increased, so did our frustration with the situation. However, the instant we could see the lobby from the stairs, the room fell silent. Shocked, we paused for a moment, and then we sped down the remaining stairs into a dark, empty room.

We were alone.

The Bar at The Brook Forest Inn
(Photo: Haunted Colorado)

We flipped on the lights. There was no sign that anyone had been there. The front doors were closed and there weren't any tracks leading up to them in the snow outside. There were no clods of snow from stomping boots on the floor, or any winter coats hanging on the coat rack. And there weren't any open bottles of wine or half-empty glasses in the bar. We examined the rooms, walked around slowly and checked every corner. If it had been summer, all we would have heard would be the sounds of crickets.

"Okay…" Bryan breathed to himself.

"Let's find out what the others heard and see if we can somehow recreate this," I suggested.

"Sure. Sounds good."

There was cautiousness in our speech, volume, and actions, like the whole party was going to jump out and scream, "PUNKED!" But that didn't happen. To be honest, we hadn't yet entertained the idea of a ghostly party. We figured there was a natural explanation; we just didn't know what it was at that point.

We ascended the stairs like zombies. When we rejoined our team members upstairs, they looked surprised.

"You must have scared the shit out of them!" one of them exclaimed. "The noise stopped suddenly."

"But *when* did you hear it stop?" Bryan asked.

"Huh? When you were coming back up the stairs."

Bryan and I threw each other a look.

"Not when we were going *down* the stairs?"

"Nope. They kept making noise until you were on your way back up the stairs. Then it sounded like someone just unplugged them."

That was really strange. They continued to hear the party *after* we went down into that silent, empty room. What was going on here? Bryan and I explained what had happened, and we all sat quietly for several minutes listening carefully for any noise coming from downstairs. There was nothing. Then we all went downstairs and searched the main floor again to prove to our team that no one was there.

In many years of investigating the Brook Forest Inn, this "ghostly" party has never repeated itself. We have recordings of the sounds of doors slamming, footsteps, hinges creaking, whistling, and various other moans and creaks but nothing that resembles the sounds we heard that cold, snowy night.

When we have strange experiences, we try to come up with a few possible explanations for what happened, even if we can't prove or recreate that experience. In this case, our theory is that we experienced an auditory illusion. This is the aural equivalent of an optical illusion in which people hear sounds that just aren't there. Snowy weather in the mountains can bring an eerie silence. It seems to breath a white noise through which we can hear sounds that are not really present. Perhaps there was a snowplow outside, or a storm, which tricked our brains into thinking we'd heard the sounds of a ghostly party.

Ultimately, we don't know what happened that night. We don't know why we all heard the distinctive sounds of a party when there was nothing there. But it is a very important thing to be able to admit, "I don't know." Sometimes it's fun to just have some wonder and mystery left in our lives. This ghostly party has puzzled us for years, but to be honest, we don't mind one little bit.

Matthew Baxter has worked as a paranormal claims investigator for several decades. He is the other half of the Bryan & Baxter duo, a kind of paranormal Penn & Teller, in which Baxter is the loud one. He has spent many years investigating businesses and private residences, reassuring people who watch too much *Ghost Hunters* that their house isn't haunted. He has recreated an alien visitation and performed exorcisms, Victorian séances, and many other crazy stunts, all in the name of science. Matthew has appeared on various television programs including "Larry King Live," "The Ten Most Terrifying Places in America," and National Geographic's "The History of UFOs." He has also given numerous talks around the country at conferences, libraries, schools, universities, and museums. www.bryanandbaxter.com

Reflections Of The Past

Hal Bidlack

I've been told my house is haunted.

As I neared the end of my 25-year military career, my wife and I bought a house off base in preparation for retirement. The house had sat on the market for about a year, unsold, in spite of being in a fine neighborhood. Our realtor explained that a young couple had built the house, and then tragically, the husband died in an accident, leaving behind his wife and small child. The widow moved out of their dream home because it was simply too painful to stay. We were touched by the story, but not fearing a curse or a haunting as other prospective buyers had, we made an offer on the house. It was accepted, and we moved in.

Due to the vagaries of military service, I ended up being posted to the U.S. Department of State in Washington D.C., leaving my wife and kids behind for, we thought, about two years before I would retire and return home. Alas, after only a few months, two events took place that shook me to my core. The first was 9/11. I happened to be in the Pentagon during the attack, and had to see and do stuff I don't want to see or do ever again. And, just about a month after that, my wife called with the news that she had been diagnosed with cancer. The military can be wonderful in such situations, and I soon found myself home permanently. Unfortunately, we lost that final battle, and Martha died in 2003.

"A second tragedy in this house," a friend remarked.

Then the ghost appeared.

My kids having left home to attend college and beyond, I was alone in the house with only the cat. One night, I sat on the couch watching TV when I saw a strange form out of the corner of my eye. It walked across the landing at the top of the stairs.

I was startled.

I saw this ghost over the course of several nights. It appeared irregularly, but always moved quickly from left to right toward our bedroom, although I never saw it when I looked for it. It was like a shadow but also like a spot of light. There was no pattern to the sightings, and it didn't make a nightly appearance.

The Landing
(Photo: Hal Bidlack)

Had I seen a ghost? I didn't know what to believe.

But there's a big difference between believing and knowing.

We "know" things that are empirically proven—facts and truths. And we "believe" things with less empirical evidence—opinions and suppositions. And therein lies the rub: People often disagree about what is true, and what is not, what is opinion and what is knowledge. We argue about what we know, and what others do not.

And, all too often, in that murky land between knowledge and belief, one finds landmines of information, which, when triggered, seem to provide "evidence" to support whatever people want to believe. This is clearly true in politics, sports and in our daily lives. It is often harmless, but not always. The nexus between belief and knowledge has fueled wars, destroyed marriages, and caused pain to many. Some find great comfort in beliefs that can't be proven, while others find loss and discomfort.

We humans are gifted with a sense of imagination—a wondrous and thrilling ability to ponder beyond our own existence. Einstein once wrote, "The true sign of intelligence is not knowledge, but imagination." The author Robert Fulghum wrote, "I believe that imagination is stronger than knowledge. That myth is more potent than history. That dreams are more powerful than facts. That hope always triumphs over experience. That laughter is the only cure for grief. And I believe that love is stronger than death."

But when it comes to our emotions, sometimes our imaginations can override our knowledge and our sense of reason.

I remember being intrigued by magician James Randi from an early age. I watched his many appearances on various TV shows, where he duplicated supposed paranormal phenomena through slight of hand and other magician's tricks. I found this fascinating, and began to try my own hand at magic. Years later, I was fortunate enough to meet and get to know the Amazing Randi as a friend and mentor. I became a member of the Board of Directors of his organization, and served as the master of ceremony for nearly all his organization's annual meetings. I became, and am proud to call myself, a skeptic—a word with multiple meanings, but to me, it means only one thing— show me proof of a claim before I will accept it.

But then, I may have seen a ghost. Back to that in a minute…

Mr. Randi famously offered a million dollars to anyone who could demonstrate the existence of the paranormal. I became involved with this Million Dollar Challenge and met people who claimed they could see through someone's body to locate damaged internal organs, people who claim to be able to find water by waving around coat hangers, and with those who say they can talk to the dead. One woman even believed she could make people pee their pants on command. Happily for our test subject, she could not.

The prize has never been claimed. Mr. Randi once said that there are two types of people who make paranormal claims—those who truly believe they have a supernatural ability, and those that know they do not, yet they prey on believers for money and fame. Only members of the first group ever applied for the million dollars. Those in the second group know they can make much more by conning people. These charlatans are evil, heartless monsters that harass those in the deepest pain, at the most difficult times in their lives—for money.

But for those with good hearts who aren't skeptics, I used to wonder how they could believe what they believed? I just didn't get it. That's why it pays to have a mentor. Mr. Randi told me that it's not about people wanting to believe in paranormal phenomena; it is that they *need* to. They ache, they hurt, and sometimes a belief in something supernatural can ease the pain and make life more livable.

Maybe that's why I kind of, sort of, saw a ghost?

There was a part of me that wanted it to be Martha; that wanted to know she was still with me. I needed to believe, after my harrowing experience in the Pentagon, and after losing the woman I had been with for 24 years. I needed things to make sense again. I needed to feel less lost, and less alone. I needed to feel less scared and less angry.

I needed to feel.

And so, I understand the need to believe. I understand why, when a comforting image or idea comes before us, that we yearn to reach out and take it. I wanted it to be real.

But, I also believe in the scientific method. I know how often we can fool ourselves. So I investigated the ghost.

One evening, I went to the part of the house where I had seen the ghost, and I waited for it to appear. After a while, a car drove down the quiet street behind my house. I noticed that when it came around the curve, its headlights swept over the condominiums across the street. If the car drove just so, the headlights reflected off a window. And when the light reflected, the motion of the car caused a flicker of light to pass, from left to right, across my hallway.

My ghost was a reflected headlight.

The mystery was solved. My house is not haunted—no ghost walks the halls. I still see the reflected light from time to time, out of the corner of my eye. And now I know what it really is.

But part of me would still like to believe.

Dr. Hal Bidlack is a retired Air Force officer. For many years he worked with the James Randi Educational Foundation as Board Member and as M.C. for the organization's annual conference, The Amaz!ng Meeting. He is currently a senior research fellow at two D.C.-based think tanks dealing with national security issues related to climate change. He holds a doctorate from the University of Michigan, focusing on environmental security concerns. He is the father of three, and grandfather of two, and currently lives in Colorado.

The Dead Letter

Matt Bille

It was 1978, and I had just returned home to Florida after completing my first summer at college.

One morning, I walked down to the mailbox to collect the mail. I opened the metal mailbox door with a key, peered inside and saw that there was only a single item—a handwritten letter that was addressed to me. When I reached inside and took it, I experienced a very sharp electrical shock. I dropped the letter to the ground and shook my hand.

At that moment I *knew* someone had died.

Okay, I didn't know it, but I had an overwhelming feeling that someone had died. I stared at the letter there on the ground, almost afraid to pick it up. But eventually I did and took it home where I placed it on the kitchen table. I kept looking at it, a sense of dread preventing me from opening it up. Finally, curiosity got the better of me. My hands shook as I slowly opened the envelope and read the letter.

Sure enough, the letter revealed that someone had died.

Most of us have experienced coincidences. Perhaps you were thinking about a long-lost friend and then you bumped into that very person in the street. Maybe the phone rang (before the days of Caller ID) and you instinctively knew who was calling. Or you and your spouse said the same thing at the same time. What about those times that you thought of a song, turned on the radio, and that very song was playing?

A close college school friend wrote the letter. She told me that her boyfriend had recently died in a horrific motorcycle accident. I felt myself tearing up as I read. I was also in shock because it seemed that I had experienced a premonition of the letter's contents.

To many people, coincidences are believed to be paranormal. But in our complex, fast-paced modern lives, they are an inevitable outcome of the countless cues and events flashing through our brains every waking moment. But what are they?

In *Methods for Studying Coincidences*, Diaconis and Mostelle say that, "A coincidence is a surprising concurrence of events, perceived as meaningfully related, with no apparent causal connection."

Sometimes we see a causal connection between events, even when there isn't one.

One day my mother awoke at 2:00 a.m. to the smell of raisin toast, which was her father's never-missed breakfast. She later found out that my paternal grandfather had died at that time. It was just a coincidence that someone in her apartment block was making raisin toast at that hour, but my mother is Catholic, and because she had never smelled raisin toast in her building before, she believed that this was God's way of allowing her father-in-law to say "Goodbye."

Coincidences surrounding death, like my experience and that of my mother, are those that we are highly likely to notice and remember because death is a milestone event. We are also prone to assign additional significance to these coincidences or even interpret them as signs.

Let's draw back from the focus on death to more mundane—yet surprising—coincidences. As an aviation buff, one story that comes to mind happened to pilot and author Richard Bach. While on a barnstorming tour, Bach watched as a friend crashed the plane he was flying. This was a 1929 Detroit-Parks P-2A Speedster, which is an extremely rare biplane (only eight were built). Amazingly, the pilot was uninjured, and his team managed to fix all of the damage sustained to the plane, except for one component—a hard-to-find strut. Without this critical spare part they were seemingly stuck. That is, until a man who owned a hangar at the field came over to help. He listened to their story and pointed to that very part in a junk pile only ten feet from where they were standing. It was sitting there in plain view. Bach reviewed the string of events and concluded, "…coincidence was a foolish answer."

1929 Detroit-Parks P-2A Speedster
(Photo: Airliners)

But was it?

Even a thorough knowledge of the laws of chance still leaves us with cases that seem so strange to those involved that psychoanalyst Carl Jung created the theory of "a meaningful coincidence," which is better known as *synchronicity*.

In the 1970s, Anthony Hopkins won a part in a movie called *The Girl From Petrovka*, which was adapted from a novel. He wanted to read the book so he set out to several bookstores. He was unable to find a copy. However, on the train ride home he spotted a book on a nearby seat. The book just happened to be a heavily annotated copy of *The Girl From Petrovka*. During the filming of the movie, Hopkins met the book's author, George Feifer, who mentioned that he had lent his own copy of the book to a friend who had lost it. Hopkins then showed Feifer the book he had found on the train and Feifer recognized this as his personal copy.

We tend to think that coincidences are meaningfully related, when they are only related by random chance.

The "Law of Truly Large Numbers" essentially says that, if a set of circumstances repeats enough times, coincidences will occur. But we can picture Bach standing there, holding that strut, and pondering the fact that the circumstances most certainly hadn't recurred often. Indeed, they had happened just once, and yet the coincidence occurred. He could have repeated that crash at every airfield in the world (not that he would want to), or Hopkins could have ridden trains for the rest of his life, and neither would have ever experienced these things again.

Throughout history, such bizarre events have been consigned to a higher power. A popular quote of unknown origin is that "Coincidence is God's way of remaining anonymous." Many cultures past and present, from the Polynesians to modern New Age movements, simply don't believe in coincidence but think that these events fulfill some sort of cosmic purpose. On the TV show "NCIS," Special Agent Leroy Jethro Gibbs calls it Rule 39: "There is no such thing as coincidence."

Observing what may at first seem like coincidence, and then finding a pattern, is an important path to learning. We are programmed by evolution to notice patterns, and for good reason. If a saber-tooth tiger sneaks up on the cave one time from the north when it's dark and the wind is from the south, then that may be a coincidence. If someone disappears every time those circumstances appear, it's a meaningful pattern with cause and effect, and one you had better learn quickly.

We may also notice the opposite: Coincidences that seem to be patterns because we aren't aware of the bigger picture. A mother may talk to three friends and discover two, like her, had children who were ill shortly after vaccinations. She may see a pattern because of the limited data set: If she could talk to fifty parents or read a study of 1,000 parents, she might realize that coincidence is at work in her immediate circle. This is a case where not understanding chance and probability leads to tragically bad decisions, as well as being a situation where people's investment is so deep and personal they don't want to recognize the proof of coincidence.

A few weeks after I read her letter, I spoke with my friend about the strange experience. She claimed to be psychic and believed that her emotions had been infused into her letter. When I touched the letter, the bad news transferred psychically to my mind.

Was it the hand of God? ESP? Telepathy? Or was it just a strange coincidence?

Whether we pay attention to them or not, coincidences are all around us. Again from Diaconis and Mosteller: "We are swimming in an ocean of coincidences. Our explanation is that nature and we ourselves are creating these, sometimes causally, and also through perception and objective accidental relationships."

Coincidences are, of course, all in the mind. We make the connections. Just as I did back in 1995 when I published my first book,

Rumors of Existence. Not only did a very small press publish the book without any publicity, but also the nationwide distributor didn't even list it. Yet far away in North Carolina, someone who had no idea who I was gifted my great-aunt with a copy of my book.

Was it just a coincidence?

Matt Bille is a science writer and novelist specializing in space history and popular zoology. He is the author of *Shadows of Existence, Rumors of Existence*, and the novel *The Dolmen*. www.mattbille.com

An Out-of-Body Experience

Susan Blackmore

In 1970, I was a psychology student at St. Hilda's College, Oxford. At that time, I was running the Oxford University Society for Psychical Research, and we used to invite mediums and psychics to give us lectures, conducted experiments with ESP cards, read about astral projection and had regular sessions with a Ouija board in my college room. As the tradition was, we wrote the letters of the alphabet on scraps of paper, along with the words 'Yes' and 'No' and the numerals 0–9, arranged them in a circle on a table and placed an upturned glass in the center. Then we all placed one finger on the glass, half closed our eyes, and began asking the spirits to appear. Typically the glass would start moving and, ever faster, spelling out answers to our questions. I guess some of us believed in spirit communication and we got terribly excited whenever a door creaked or a curtain moved with no sign of a breeze, but we were also skeptical and curious to find out the truth.

On the night of Sunday, November 8, a group of us had been having a session with a Ouija board. We were exhausted, so the others left, and I went with my friends Kevin and Vicki to her room to smoke some hash. After a few minutes, I began to feel disconnected from the others. Then I started hallucinating. We were listening to music, but hearing it was almost akin to sight and I could see colors. I thought this was just part of the drug experience. In my mind, I began to move through brightly colored tunnels. This went on for half an hour and then the transition came. I suddenly realized I was rising up towards the ceiling and gently drifting about. I looked down on my own body. Had I not been smoking pot I would have been worried by this, however, now it didn't concern me at all. I continued to look at myself with interest and enjoyed the strange sensations.

I closed my eyes and they remained shut for most of the time. If I opened them nothing I saw made any sense. I could still hear the music and the others talking but they seemed so far away. Vicki asked if I'd like some coffee but I couldn't answer, so she left the room.

Now alone with me, Kevin asked, "Where are you, Sue?"

I told him I was floating above the room and I explained what I could see. It was like I was watching a movie and describing the picture to someone who couldn't see it. From that time I continued talking, almost continuously, for the next three hours. Now that I was speaking and not alone I found the confidence to explore the room. I didn't think it at all strange that I could be above my body and yet still in control of the body below and able to speak through it. And everything seemed real. Looking down from the ceiling felt as real, even more real, than looking out through my eyes had seemed all my life.

St. Hilda's College, Oxford University
(Photo: St. Hilda's College)

Then I saw a silver cord coming from where my tummy should be. It was shiny white, and slowly bending and moving. I reached out my hand to touch it and discovered that if I wanted a hand I could have one, or as many as I liked, although it wasn't necessary to have a hand at all. I could move the cord at will, and had great fun doing so. I looked harder at the cord and saw that it entered my physical body at the neck. There appeared to be no head on the body. It was just the shape of my body and I was made of the same kind of whitish moving stuff of which the cord was made. With Kevin's encouragement, I set off to explore the world outside.

I whizzed out of the room and into the night sky. I was astral traveling. I saw below me all the roofs of the buildings in Oxford. I think I knew they weren't the roofs I should have seen, were I really there, but to me they represented the roofs of St. Hilda's. I became aware that I was moving away quickly but it wasn't clear where I was going, nor did I have any conscious control over it. I didn't take much notice of where I was going until I was suddenly aware that I was somewhere near the Mediterranean. I am not sure how I knew this, but it seemed quite obvious at the time. I saw an island below and thought I should take a closer look at it. As a consequence of this thought, I found myself closing in on the island.

As I approached the island I could see its outline, but the shape seemed to be changing all the time and pulsating with the music I could still hear. I tried to describe to the others what I was seeing as I grew closer. At this point, I discovered what was to be of such importance later on—I could change shape at will. So far, I was aware that I could produce hands at will, but now I was able to lose my bodily shape altogether. I could become any shape I wanted, so I stretched out flat over the island. Then I thought my way down in among the trees on the island. For the first time I became scared as I thought the cord might get tangled up and damaged in the trees. However, I soon found that it could pass among or through the trees with no difficulty whatsoever. I then became scared again because it was dark and dank among the trees and I feared I might never escape. Feelings of pleasure and displeasure were very exaggerated and the feeling of being in that thick darkness was intense. As soon as I discovered that I could move up again at will, I lost my sense of fear and enjoyed darting into and out of the trees.

I made my first conscious decision to leave the island, but I was still unable either to control where I was going or to try to go somewhere specific. Soon, I saw that I was traveling over Europe. Again, I don't really know how I could tell where I was, but from a long way up the outline looked like a map. I thought I went over Italy, Switzerland and then France. I moved over the sea and immediately wanted to go down to it. I gradually got closer to the sea and to the land. I tried to get right down to the water and had the rather pleasant experience of floating above the water, being lifted and buffeted by the waves. I arrived at a beach and after some difficulty I landed on the sand and looked around. Again I got a little scared because I was down below very high cliffs and I couldn't see how to get out. As soon as I tried to move I found that I didn't have to climb the rocky cliffs but could simply arrive at the top instantaneously. All I had to do was think of something or somewhere and I would be there.

Yet there were oddities about this 'travelling by thought'. If I looked down I moved upwards and if I looked up I moved down. But to move horizontally I had to look where I wanted to go. For shorter distances I could just imagine where I wanted to be and arrive there almost instantly or in short hops. For longer distances, I flew way high up and at great speed but with very little control.

I decided that I'd try to travel back to Oxford. Whether this decision was prompted by fear, curiosity, or a desire to get back into my body, I don't know. However, I was soon back in the room where Vicki and Kevin were still patiently listening to my rantings.

My body's eyes opened.

"Hello," said Kevin.

"Hello," I replied.

"So, you're really here?"

"Yes. I'm really here," I confirmed. Then, "Goodbye," I said, and left again.

I found during this brief return to my body that I could see with my own eyes, but what I did see didn't make much sense. The conflict with my inner vision was too great. So, reassured that I could get back if I wanted to, I set off travelling again. This time I decided consciously that I'd like to go to somewhere that I had been to previously, to see if it looked the same. I chose to visit New York City, and very quickly I found myself there. All my movements were becoming more deliberate and much faster, even my unintentional movements were now much faster than before. I arrived in New York and it was sunny. I moved as a large, almost ellipsoid shape, over the buildings until I came to the top of 5th Avenue. I shot down to street level, where I became much smaller. After taking a quick look at the cars and people, which I couldn't see as clearly as I'd have expected, I became frightened. This was the first time I had been really afraid and it was a struggle to be able to think my way up the buildings to emerge in space again. When I was between the skyscrapers I could move up and down quite easily.

I had no clear idea of where I wanted to go next. I soon found myself heading, ever faster, towards South America. There, I amused myself in the childish pastime of using the coastline as a giant slide. The curly bit at the southern tip of the continent was the end of the slide and from there I shot round the bend and up into the air before landing in the Atlantic Ocean. This was tremendously exciting and I laughed as I described my adventure to Vicki and Kevin. I wanted to ride the slide again, so I did.

Then I headed towards England again. I arrived in Oxford and went back to the room where my body was. This time I could not get into my body at all, at least not as I had almost done before. I was only able to hover over it although what I could see was much clearer. I could see Vicki and Kevin very clearly but when I looked at my own body I was shocked. It was a strange brown color, shaded almost like a drawing, and not much like me at all. There was a jagged edge around the neck where the head had been and I found myself landing on it, like a fly, before slipping down inside. I swooped about inside, exploring what seemed to be an empty shell, and zooming up and down the legs and into the feet.

Apparently, I was making so much noise that Vicki ordered me to shut up. The urgent tone in her voice made the visual image of an elephant appear. It upset me and I soon found myself hovering above my body again.

"Take that body away," I said to Vicki. "I know you don't like it. Why don't you take it down to its own room? I can't move it, you take it away."

I kept referring to myself as "that body." I had lost any sense that this body was really mine or that I could control it.

I suppose it was the desire to get back to normal that led to me trying to get bigger, to fill up that empty shell and regain control. But this attempt failed spectacularly. Instead of growing to the right size and taking control of my body again I simply grew and grew and kept on growing. I expanded out through the room and through my friends, through the building and the streets, through the underground places of Oxford, and ultimately the earth. I became larger than the whole earth quite quickly, and had the experience of being able to look at the earth while I was all round it. I didn't stop there. I got bigger and bigger and incorporated the moon. From there, I expanded through the planets of the entire solar system. Then came our whole galaxy and, as I was moving and expanding faster and faster, I had soon enveloped many other galaxies. Finally, there was nowhere further to go. I had reached what I took to be the limit of the universe—however silly that sounds now!

Kevin was concerned and started asking questions. What was I doing? Could I see anything else? What came next? As I struggled to answer it seemed like I was clambering through some kind of mist or cloud to gain the slightest glimpse of another world. I saw two shiny white cliffs above me with an opening between them that lead up to a kind of sky. It was a real effort to get up those cliffs, like fighting against something intangible, almost like swimming against a current, always achieving a little but then slipping back and only just hanging on. I got a very brief glimpse at the top. What I "saw" was indescribable in three-dimensional terms, but was like hundreds of eyes, or one huge eye, staring at me from every direction at once. Not that it seemed to take any notice of me. Then I slipped back.

I was exhausted and could take no more. Vicki was longing to get rid of me and go to bed but there was no way I could just snap back to normal. With Kevin constantly urging me on I struggled to get back into my body. At first it seemed easy but as soon as I opened my eyes I seemed to shoot out of the body again and end up wherever I had been looking. Then I had to start again and get back in, try again, fail, try again. Corners presented a special challenge, as I seemed unable to understand how three dimensions could meet in one place. I kept talking to myself, saying, "Wherever you go you have to take the body with you," and, "You can only be in one place at a time." Then gradually, after about three quarters of an hour, I finally got to the point where I was inside my body and I could see with my eyes alone.

I stood up carefully. The room looked very strange and so did the others. So did my own body. Looking down at myself I could still see the whitish stuff I was made of. It was more or less coincident with my body but not quite and still moving slightly. Surrounding the others was a similar pale glow, as though they too had another body or a living aura. Further out than that was another body that I could feel with my hands but not see. Was this the occultists' aura that psychics could see and other people could not? Had my third eye been opened?

I played around with these sensations for some time before cautiously taking a few steps and setting off back to my own room.

Kevin thought that it would be dangerous to go to sleep because my astral body might leave and be unable to return. So he kept me awake until well into the next morning. I did finally sleep and as far as I know my astral body did nothing of the kind. But I felt very weird indeed. As I cycled around Oxford I seemed to be watching myself from one side and almost fell off my bike. In a tutorial two days later my rather strict tutor told me to pull myself together and pay attention. According to my diary, she said, "You seem to be floating off on a cloud somewhere," and I blurted out, "I am!" Then I felt I had to give some kind of explanation. She seemed genuinely interested, so I told her more or less all about it, until she eventually said we were rather stupid to be messing around with drugs at such an unstable age.

So that was the mysterious experience that changed my life. That was the experience whose memory kept nudging me for decades to come, reminding me that I didn't understand, making me dissatisfied with our scientific understanding of the world and the mind. That was the experience that kept me asking questions and more questions. It still does.

Dr. Susan Blackmore is a freelance writer, lecturer and broadcaster, and a Visiting Professor at the University of Plymouth. She has a degree in psychology and physiology from Oxford University and an MSc and a Ph.D. in parapsychology from the University of Surrey. She no longer works on the paranormal. Her current research interests include memes, evolutionary theory, consciousness, and meditation. She is a TED lecturer, blogs for *The Guardian*, and often appears on radio and television. Dr. Blackmore's books include *Beyond the Body: An Investigation of Out-of-the-Body Experiences; Dying to Live: Science and the Near-death Experience; The Meme Machine*, and *Conversations on Consciousness*. This story is adapted from her latest book, *Seeing Myself: The New Science of Out-of-Body Experiences.*
www.susanblackmore.co.uk

The Writers' Retreat At The Haunted Mansion

S.G. Browne

I'm driving along a two-lane, winding mountain road with two other writers, Eunice and Loren. The three of us are headed to a writers' retreat at a supposedly haunted mansion located up in the hills above a small, quaint town in Northern California. A primary condition of the invitation is that none of us are allowed to mention its name or location outside of the retreat: The proprietors don't want the publicity.

We drive up the narrow, twisting road lined with trees that form a canopy above us, the leaves red and yellow and orange with the burgeoning colors of autumn.

"It's so beautiful," Loren says. "I love this time of year."

Eunice looks out the windows. "I think it's spooky. Like a scene out of a movie: The unsuspecting writers driving to the haunted mansion for a weekend retreat, unaware of what awaits."

I'm dubious of the whole "haunted house" thing. While I'm open to the possibility of the existence of ghosts, I've never encountered one. In fact, I've never had any kind of supernatural experience. So I'm not expecting anything to happen this weekend. At least not to me.

As we drive, the three of us talk about our favorite haunted house movies: *The Legend of Hell House, House on Haunted Hill,* and *The Haunting.*

"Not the remake but the old version," Eunice says. "I especially love that line, 'In the night. In the dark.' Very spooky."

"You're kind of big on spooky," I say.

"I'm a horror writer," Eunice says. "What do you expect?"

When we finally make it to the top of the hill, the trees part and the mansion appears in front of us. But rather than the dark, foreboding manse conjured up by our imaginations, the place is friendly and inviting, with a large front lawn shaped like a heart.

"Nothing particularly scary about that," I say.

After unloading our bags, the three of us check in with the hostess of the retreat—a dark poet named Rain with Bukowskian tendencies who takes us on a tour of the mansion. There are only a dozen or so writers attending this retreat and most of them won't arrive until later, so with three floors of rooms to choose from, there are more than enough for each of us to have our own. But Eunice, a burned-out middle school teacher from southern California, doesn't want to sleep by herself.

"Does anyone really want to sleep by themselves?" she asks.

"I do," Loren says.

Eunice convinces me to share a room with her, so I pick a large one that faces the front of the house overlooking the heart-shaped lawn. But Eunice suggests a different one on the side of the house that has a fireplace and its own bathroom. It has two other doors: One next to the bathroom that opens into the hall, and a second door with frosted glass panes that connects to another room. Twin beds rest opposite the fireplace, heads against the wall. Eunice takes the one closest to the bathroom.

Later, after the other writers have arrived and we've all eaten a delicious homemade dinner, the sun begins to set and several of us go out to explore the grounds and get the lay of the land. You know those people in horror movies who go walking into the woods at night, picking their way along unlit paths with flashlights in hand, down to the creepy pond where two people have allegedly drowned? You just *know* that something bad is going to happen. You'd think as writers (especially horror writers) we would be smart enough not to fall into the same pattern.

To be fair, the people who drowned decades ago were apparently drunk at a party with no lifeguard on duty. So it's not like there was anything supernatural about their deaths. But when you're spending the weekend at a haunted mansion, you'd think playing it safe would be the smart thing to do. For instance, walking back from the haunted pond the same way we'd come, which was the familiar and safest way, rather than taking a different path that leads around the back of the mansion.

A narrow path with a steep drop off. A path with rocks and weeds that make the footing more treacherous.

That path.

So when we see the strange wooden totem that looks like something out of *The Blair Witch Project* dangling from a tree, it's probably best to just notice it's there and comment on how creepy it is rather than walking up to it and touching it, just to prove that nothing bad will happen. And when we discover the meditation area located in a grove of trees with a stone table that we all agree looks more like a table used for ritualistic sacrifices than a nice spot for a picnic, you'd think we would refrain from taking turns laying on the table and pretending to be dead. Maybe we're just using humor to balance out our unspoken fear. Maybe we know we're safe and sound since this is real life and not a horror movie and even if the mansion is haunted there's nothing that can hurt us. Not really.

In bed later that night I stare up at the ceiling, the swollen rays of the moon spilling in through the bedroom window. An anemic glow of artificial light filters through the frosted glass panes of the door near my bed. I can make out the silhouettes of furniture in the room, and the fireplace on the opposite wall, and my suitcase sitting next to my bed. I can see the shape of Eunice in her bed, beneath the covers, lightly snoring.

There are voices in the hallway. Indistinct murmurs. I'm not sure if the voices belong to members of the staff or to some of the other writers or if it's just my imagination stirred up by the stories about this place. Stories about beds freshly made one moment and then all of the covers pulled down the next. And of a phantom hand brushing the hair from someone's forehead. And a shadowy image drifting along the third floor hallways.

We had gone on a ghost hunt earlier in the evening using Electro-Magnetic Field meters to help detect the presence of ghosts. The EMF meters found activity in various spots throughout the house, but I had doubted these were ghosts. More likely these were false positives caused by electrical wiring in the walls. But on three separate occasions and with three separate EMF meters, we had found electromagnetic activity in our very bedroom, near the fireplace, with the meters spiking all the way to red. Yet no electrical wiring could be found.

In my bed, in the darkness, I study that fireplace. Then I glance around at the other shadows in the room. I've never seen a ghost. But it seems like everyone else at the retreat has had some kind of supernatural encounter. Even Eunice. "It's not something you want to happen to you," she'd say. But that's all she'll say about it.

I roll on to my side and look at the clock on the bedside table. It reads 11:45 p.m. Eunice's light snoring continues, and I try to follow her lead. But no sooner do I close my eyes than I sense the air growing thick and heavy, as if something is descending upon me. But when I open my eyes, there's nothing there.

After a few moments I close my eyes again and listen to the faint voices in the hallway, to Eunice's night sounds and to the house settling. Eventually I fall asleep.

A creak of the wooden floor and the sound of a door closing brings me fully awake again. I open my eyes and stare into the darkness, watching, listening. But all is quiet again. I notice that the bathroom door is shut. I thought it was open when I went to sleep but now I can't remember. I glance at Eunice in the other bed, though I don't hear her snoring anymore. At least I think it's Eunice. Now all I can make out is a shape beneath the covers.

I try to convince myself that the sound of the door closing was someone coming into our room to use the bathroom, but I don't see any light from beneath its door. I continue watching the bathroom door, and listening to the house, which has grown silent. After a few moments I realize I'm holding my breath.

The clock by my bed now says 2:13 a.m. Next to the clock is the EMF meter I had used on the ghost hunt. I think about how it spiked near our fireplace, and wonder what would happen if I turned it on now. I think about picking it up and waving it around to see if it registers anything. But when I'm about to do just that the bathroom door opens. Anthony, one of the other writers, walks out of the bathroom, leaves the bedroom, and closes the door behind him.

I roll on to my back and listen, waiting to see if there are any creaks or whispers before I close my eyes. Again, I have that sense of the air growing thick and heavy, as if someone is leaning over me. But when I open my eyes, the oppressiveness vanishes and there's just the furniture and the shadows and the shape of Eunice beneath her covers. I stare at the bedroom door for several more minutes before I close my eyes and wait to see if the atmosphere around me changes again. When it doesn't, I relax, and eventually drift off to sleep.

The Bedroom
(Photo: S.G. Browne)

I'm not sure if something wakes me or if I was already awake because it seems like I've been on the edge of sleep all night long. But I thought I heard a noise in the hallway. I look again at the bathroom door and the door to the hallway, waiting to see if one of them opens, listening for the sound of footsteps. But the only sound is Eunice's deep breathing. The clock says 4:54 a.m. Closing my eyes, I try to get in a couple hours of sleep before dawn.

And then again, the air grows heavy. Only this time it's thicker, denser, as if someone is almost upon me. I'm not sure what happens first: If I open my eyes or if I feel the hand on my left shoulder. I'm being shaken, hard and fast. But no one is there.

The space next to my bed looks hazy, like the air over hot pavement. There's a definite shape to it but I can't quite make it out. My eyes won't move. I can't shift my gaze up or down. I can't move my head or my arms or my legs either. It's as if I'm paralyzed.

I open my mouth to call out. To cry, "Hey!" just to let someone know what's happening to me, to try to break the spell. But I can't speak. I can't move. I can't make a sound. All I can do is stare, my mouth open and my eyes wide as I try to break free from whatever is shaking me.

I'm hyper aware of everything. I feel my tongue against my teeth and the dry roof of my mouth and my heart pounding in my chest. I see the bedroom door and my suitcase and the edge of the bed. I feel the mattress under me and the sheets against my skin. I'm not asleep. I'm not in that strange space halfway between sleep and consciousness. I'm wide awake. I'm the most awake I've ever been in my life.

I don't know how long the shaking goes on. Five seconds. Ten. Half a minute. But then it suddenly stops. Either that or I finally manage to break the spell and sit up, wide-eyed, and look around the room. When I finally find my voice, I cry out, "Motherfucker!"

From the bedside table I grab the EMF meter and turn it on, waving it from side to side, measuring the electromagnetic field, expecting to see it spike up to red. But the meter remains green. Whatever was shaking me is gone.

My first reaction is to think I imagined the whole thing, that I was asleep or somewhere in between. But I know I was awake and that it wasn't my imagination.

With the EMF meter clutched tightly in my hand, I lay back down. I glance at the space next to my bed where the shimmering shape had been. What was it? What had it wanted? Was it just having fun, or did it intend something more nefarious? Whatever the answers, I wonder if it will return, and if it does, if I'll experience the same paralysis as before. I wonder if I'll be more prepared for it the next time.

I wonder if it will follow me home.

S.G. Browne is an author of dark comedy and social satire. His novels include *Breathers; Fated; Lucky Bastard; Big Egos*, and *Less Than Hero,* as well as the short story collection *Shooting Monkeys in a Barrel* and the heartwarming holiday novella *I Saw Zombies Eating Santa Claus.* He's an ice cream connoisseur, Guinness aficionado, cat enthusiast, and a sucker for *It's a Wonderful Life.* He currently lives in San Francisco. www.sgbrowne.com

Out Standing In My Field

Brian Brushwood

Is it possible that I have lived a past life?

My earliest memory is intense and powerful—but I don't know if it is even real.

In this memory I am standing in a beautiful sunlit field of wheat. It's that golden hour shortly before sunset when everything takes on a gold-colored sheen as far as the eye can see. There is an old wooden barn in the distance and a family gathering going on. There are people around me who are laughing and talking while children throw a ball back and forth. I don't know what year this is, but it feels like somewhere between the late 1800s to the early 1900s.

"Wheat Field" by Darko Topalski
(Image: Topalski Fine Arts Gallery)

Even amidst the noise and chaos of an event such as a large family gathering, we can experience inward moments of silence and self-reflection. It was as though I was having one of those moments when something grabbed my attention. I saw the sun over the waves of grain, and although I continued looking at that exact spot, I was pulled out of the field. Suddenly, instead of being *a part of* that scene, I was now *looking at* that very same scene in a framed picture hanging on my mother's bedroom wall.

For me, there is no lead up to this memory. There is no "before." My earliest memory begins with me standing there in that field and ends with me standing in my mother's bedroom.

I was about 3 at the time of this memory, but it has stuck with me my entire life. To this day, I feel very sentimental about it. It is as though the place I was in was made of nostalgia. The recollection is always bittersweet, as if I was leaving something behind.

Another strange detail is that I still felt like I was myself standing there in that field. I was a toddler and had a sense of my identity. I wasn't suddenly a peasant boy that knew that field from having to harvest the grain every fall, or a soldier who had just returned from battle. I was still Brian Brushwood.

As I grew older, I became very interested in the occult and the supernatural and I read a lot about these topics. In my research I stumbled across theories about reincarnation, past lives, and past life regression. I recalled my memory of standing in that field of wheat and wondered if my experience was real.

Was I really there? Did it really happen?

I have held onto this memory for forty years and tell it to very few people. Memories fade and become cloudy over time if you don't do something to document them. That time came when I was invited to contribute to this book.

I now know that human memory is notoriously unreliable, and often our memories are simply wrong. Past life regression therapy has been discredited. Memories "recovered" during this therapy are not from a past life but instead from *this life*, patched together from our real life experiences and our imaginations. Repressed memory therapists can even implant false memories, unintentionally or intentionally, by using hypnosis, suggestion, and leading question techniques. This kind of therapy created the moral panic of the 1980s in which there were widespread allegations of the existence of a satanic cult that molested, tortured, and murdered children. No hard evidence for this so-called satanic ritual abuse has ever been found. Repressed memory therapy is also to blame for "memories" of alien abduction and past lives.

Of course, my "past life memory" wasn't remembered on a therapist's couch. I was only a child, so I wonder if what I experienced was instead a hallucination. It is not uncommon, or abnormal, for children to experience hallucinations. It's well known that many children have imaginary friends and invent elaborate fantasies. Perhaps I just imagined myself into that scene on the wall.

Even knowing these possible explanations, when I recall that memory it seems like I was in a different time and a different place. And then somehow I returned to the present through a cheesy 1970s landscape painting hanging on the wall in my mother's room. But I don't know exactly where my vivid memory comes from and I don't think that I ever will.

This reminds me of another strange memory, but I can explain this one. When I was a kid we had a portrait hanging on the wall of my younger brother Jay who was about three years old in the photo. It was taken at one of those studio portrait places. You could see a park in the background—if you were to look at it now, it would be obvious that it was a background image common in those studios. However, when we were growing up, both Jay and I were *convinced* that it was a candid shot taken when we were at the park one day. As we remembered it, he was running away from us and we shouted, "Hey Jay!" He spun around with a surprised look on his face and we took this picture. Looking at the photo you can almost see why a kid might believe that constructed memory. Even today, although we know the truth, my brother and I can both still retrieve that false memory and tell you everything about that day at the park...that never happened!

Reincarnation is a central belief of several eastern religions, including Hinduism and Buddhism, and it became popular in the western world with the New Age movement. Over the years I've read many stories about people who believe they have had past lives. One popular story is about a three-year-old boy from Israel who remembers being killed with an axe in a past life. In his current life he led the village elders to his buried body that revealed a head wound; he found the murder weapon and even identified his killer—who later confessed to his wicked crime. Sure, on the surface this sounds pretty amazing, but so many details of this story are missing. The events probably didn't happen this way. Maybe they never even happened at all.

Maybe my "memory" never happened either.

But when I read about these other stories of reincarnation, I realize that everyone else seems to have led really exciting past lives. They were pioneers, soldiers, famous actors, knights or kings, while many people believe they were Napoleon, Cleopatra, or Marie Antoinette.

In my "past life" I just stood in a field of wheat.

Brian Brushwood began his career in magic to get free drinks at bars and impress his friends. Now he hammers nails into his head, reads minds, and eats fire in his *Bizarre Magic* stage show that has been labeled "America's Number One College Magic Show." He is the author of *Cheats, Cons, Swindles & Tricks: 57 Ways to Scam a Free Drink; The Professional's Guide to Fire Eating*, and *Scam School: Your Guide to Scoring Free Drinks, Doing Magic and Becoming the Life of the Party*. An Internet and TV personality, Brian is a co-host of the podcasts Weird Things, Cordkillers, and Night Attack, and is the star of "Scam School" and National Geographic Channel's "Hacking the System." www.shwood.com

I, Faith Healer

Steve Cuno

My excuse is that I was 17.

If you have ever lived with a 17-year-old, or perhaps even been one for a while, you know that saying "I was 17" is tantamount to saying, "I was functioning at a maximum level of self-absorption." I entertained the notion that I was special, that there must be some world-changing purpose to my existence. Not terribly popular at school, I yearned to fit in somewhere, anywhere. Like many teens, I had a need to rebel; trouble was, I didn't have it in me to rebel in a time-honored, respectable way like failing school, breaking the law, or knocking up the girl next door. (As if. She was way out of my league. I was self-absorbed, not delusional.) In short, I suffered from typical teenage angst, the kind that normal people outgrow sooner or later.

I most likely would have outgrown it too, if I hadn't played the baritone horn. It was in the Reno High School band that I became smitten with a flute player who happened to be a Mormon. Desperate for her to talk to me, I shushed my atheist self and, feigning sincerity, uttered the fateful words, "Tell me about your religion."

Although our relationship was not fated to last, my interest in Mormonism grew genuine. What the Mormons told me appealed to my ego. They said I was chosen, that I had a purpose. They welcomed me. And when my newfound affiliation horrified family and friends, it satisfied my need to rebel while remaining a pathologically straight arrow.

I officially joined the Mormon Church on the day after my nineteenth birthday. Before long, I began saving toward becoming a full-time Mormon missionary. At age 21, off I went. The church put me through its intensive, nine-week language course and then plopped me in the Province of Québec, Canada. I spent the next two years ringing French Canadians' doorbells, telling all who neglected to slam the door fast enough that they ought to become Mormons.

Mormon missionaries live and work in pairs called "companionships." One sunny June day in a Montreal suburb, my companion and I rapped our knuckles upon the door of Jacqueline and Sam. Jacqueline answered, invited us in, and told us she was searching for "the true church." Telling a Mormon, especially a Mormon missionary, that you're searching for the true church is like dressing up as a sirloin steak and ringing a large bell in front of Pavlov's dog. Doing our best not to drool all over our neckties and name-tags, we told her that the true church was exactly what we happened to represent, pulled out our visual aids, and launched into one of our memorized lessons. Jacqueline decided almost at once that the Mormon Church was the real deal. Remarkably, Sam agreed, even though at the time church doctrine barred him from ordination to its priesthood on account of his being black. We learned that we had snatched the two from the jaws of the Jehovah's Witnesses, which mightily displeased their JW friends and mightily pleased us. Not that we gloated. Much.

We visited Jacqueline and Sam every few days, alternating between delivering the next lesson in the queue and just saying hello. It was during one of those visits that Jacqueline told us about the tumor.

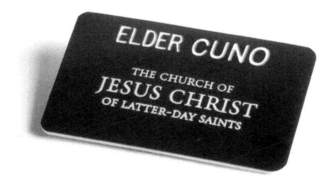

(Image: Matthew Baxter)

It was in her neck. It was big. Not just painful, it didn't let her turn her head left or right, or lift her arms higher than her shoulders. Earlier that week, her doctor recommended surgery, but Jacqueline declined. She told him she would have her missionaries give her a blessing—and heal her—instead.

If you want to unleash a torrent of excuses, ask someone who believes in miracles to produce one. Apparently Jesus oversimplified when he said, "If ye have faith as a grain of mustard seed, ye shall say unto this mountain, Remove hence to yonder place; and it shall remove; and nothing shall be impossible unto you." (KJV Matthew 17:20) It turns out that miracle-doing is not without a few caveats. First, there's the "If" in "*If* ye have faith as a grain of mustard seed." Coming up with a mustard seed's worth of faith is a lot harder than it sounds, which is why you don't see mountains removing hence to yonder place all that often. Another complication is that you're not supposed to ask for miracles in the first place. "A wicked and adulterous generation seeketh after a sign," Jesus told his disciples, just before listing signs and miracles he wanted them to look for. (Mark 16:4–18) And there's the whole "God's will" thing. If God likes a mountain where it is, not even faith the size of an avocado seed will move it. You never know when God will have a mind of his own, dismiss a request as wicked and adulterous, or stay his hand because some slacker tried to slide by with three-quarters of a mustard seed.

I thought Jacqueline would ask my companion rather than me to pronounce the blessing, since he had been a missionary longer and was more experienced. No such luck. For whatever reason, Jacqueline asked me to handle it. That should have terrified me. It should have sent myriad excuses ricocheting around inside my head. It did not. I felt surprisingly calm.

Well acquainted with the drill for Mormon blessings by this time, Jacqueline handed us a newly purchased bottle of olive oil. Yes, olive oil. Placing our fingers on the bottle, my companion and I offered a prayer to consecrate the oil for anointing the sick. First we removed the cap, because if you don't remove the cap, you're consecrating the bottle, not the oil, which obviously isn't going to do anyone any good.

Jacqueline placed a chair in the center of the living room and sat down. My companion rubbed a drop of oil on the crown of her head and uttered the perfunctory, "I anoint you with this oil which has been consecrated for the blessing of the sick." Then we gently rested our hands palms-down on her head, closed our eyes, and bowed our heads. It was time for me to get on with the blessing.

Somewhere outside a dog barked. *Don't let it distract you,* I told myself. I drew a deep breath and then started in with the usual introductory stuff. "The Lord loves you," I said. "He is pleased with you. He has heard your prayers." So much for the easy part. I'd had no idea what I would say from there. I certainly hadn't planned on commanding Jacqueline "by authority of the Melchizedek Priesthood and in the name of Jesus Christ" to be healed, or on commanding the tumor to disappear. Yet that is exactly what I overhead myself say before wrapping up with the standard "... in the name of Jesus Christ, amen."

After a suitable reverential pause, my companion and I opened our eyes. We removed our hands from Jacqueline's head.

Jacqueline rose and faced us, her eyes glistening.

She rotated her head, first far to the right, then far to the left.

She lifted her arms high over her head.

No pain.

On our next visit, Jacqueline reported that her doctor was amazed. No more tumor.

I believed we had witnessed a miracle. I kept the experience largely to myself. It was sacred to me, not something to vaunt but to treasure. To take credit or boast would have required a feat of ego beyond even my ability. I lacked the faith to heal, and I knew it. If anyone besides God deserved credit, I believed it was Jacqueline. It was she who had the faith to be healed.

Fifteen years after completing my missionary service, I no longer believed in the Mormon Church. Leaving Mormonism is no small matter, especially when you live in the Salt Lake City area, and even more so when your spouse is Mormon. My wife, Paula, who was fast succumbing to breast cancer, despaired that in eternity she would become a polygamous wife of some stranger who had remained valiant in mortality. It was no idle speculation on her part; that really is Mormon doctrine.

Most of my neighbors and friends were Mormon. Many began avoiding me lest I contaminate them. There were rumors that I had committed grave sins that I was unwilling to make right. Some accused me of pride, a hot topic at the time for Mormons, especially for those who were proud of not being proud. Some went so far as to suggest that I, horror of horrors, was *an intellectual*, which had recently become a bad thing. This was thanks to a Mormon apostle who said the biggest dangers to the church were "... the gay-lesbian movement and the feminist movement ... and the ever-present challenge from the so-called scholars or intellectuals."

Within a few years of Paula's death, I discovered scientific skepticism and logical argument. It wasn't long before I re-became an atheist, albeit a better informed, more active one this time around.

From my new perspective, it was inevitable that I would sooner or later revisit Jacqueline's blessing and ask myself, *what really happened on that day?*

The answer is: I don't know. Maybe it was a spontaneous recovery. They are rare, but not unknown. Their coincidence at the moment of a religious exercise is surely more rare.

But when I review the facts that I have and, more important, the facts that I don't have, I see no need to invoke that explanation. We saw no material evidence of a tumor; we knew only that Jacqueline *said* she had one. She didn't have us feel the lump in her neck. I'm not complaining, mind you, for my tummy tends not to do well with things squishy. That we saw no x-rays isn't surprising, since they would have remained at the doctor's office, but what *is* surprising is that Jacqueline made no mention of them. If her doctor truly had recommended surgery, he certainly would first have taken x-rays, and x-rays would have attested to Jacqueline's claims. Her omission of so important a detail could mean that there were no x-rays, and that no surgery had been recommended.

None of which is to suggest that Jacqueline lied. It's not unusual for people to self-diagnose, and even embellish, explanations of aches and pains. Jacqueline may have had a garden-variety stiff neck and *assumed* she had a tumor. Or she may have remembered her own concerns expressed in the doctor's office as the doctor's own words. And after the blessing, she could have turned her head and raised her arms simply by rallying herself to it.

I have no reason to doubt Jacqueline's sincerity. I have fond memories of her, Sam, and their children. I think Jacqueline truly believed she had a tumor that vanished in the course of the blessing. But her view of what happened requires a miracle or, at the very least, a rare, incredibly timed spontaneous recovery. My revised, mundane view requires only human foibles, which are neither miraculous nor rare.

Odds are there was no tumor.

These days, I use olive oil for cooking.

Steve Cuno is a marketing and advertising professional. He is the author of two books on marketing and the as-told-to author of Joanne Hanks's sardonic memoir, *It's Not About the Sex My Ass: Confessions of an Ex-Mormon, Ex-Polygamist, Ex-Wife.* Guess which book is the commercial success. In his spare time, Steve likes to read, walk his dogs, pound away on his piano, and force people to look at photos of his grandchildren. www.stevecuno.com

Ouija Bored

S. Von Cyburg

Spirits make poor conversationalists. Loath to speak up so that not-dead people can hear them, they work through intermediaries like psychics. Even then, they remain vague until you indicate that the psychic is onto something. They might prompt the psychic to ask, "Does the letter K mean anything to you?" You dig through your memory, come up with a great aunt twice removed, thrice removed if you count death as a form of removal, and recall that she really liked eating Special K cereal. With that tidbit of encouragement, the spirit who a moment earlier could only offer something vaguely K-like suddenly gushes specifics. "She's happy," the psychic relays, "and she doesn't want you to worry about her. She's sitting on a cloud with a bowl of Special K in one hand and a spoon in the other, catching up between mouthfuls with your other deceased relatives. Oh, and she says you're going on a trip sometime, you'll meet someone interesting, and someday you'll get a job that pays more. What's that? You're unemployed? There you have it. The next job will for sure pay more than you're making now. Speaking of pay, that'll be $150."

Spirits are no less vague when they conceal messages in tea leaves, tarot cards, and runes. Even more frustrating are spirits who, instead of trying to communicate something useful, content themselves with shaking the table or spewing ectoplasm (which is really difficult to get out of a shirt.) Least helpful of all are spirits who take every question for an impromptu recital request and oblige you by flying around the room, invisible, blatting on trumpets and shaking tambourines.

A breakthrough came in the late nineteenth century when spirits learned how to spell, and the "talking board" was born. About the size of a small serving tray, talking boards were bedecked with the words "yes" and "no," the letters of the alphabet, and the numbers one through nine. The spirits spelled out words by sliding a thin, roughly three-inch by five-inch piece of wood on tiny legs from one letter to the next. The thin piece of wood was called a *planchette*, most likely because that sounded decidedly more spirit-y than the English "small plank." Two or more participants would lightly rest the fingers of both hands on the planchette, ask a question, and let the spirits take it from there. The planchette would leap to life, zipping about the board and spelling out answers as it dragged surprised participants' hands along for the ride. It might have been more impressive had the spirits moved the planchette without human hands, but apparently spirits have rules, and apparently four hands minimum per planchette is one of them.

Talking boards grew in popularity. Before long, toy manufacturers began marketing them as novelties. The best known of these was the Parker Brothers Ouija board.

I first encountered a Ouija board at a friend's party. We were only 14, yet even today I am at loss to explain the wonder I witnessed that night: Namely, that someone had actually invited me to a party. As for the Ouija board, I didn't for a moment suspect that otherworldly powers were at play. I believed in no such thing. Forty years would pass before I would stumble upon the term *ideomotor response;* but even then it seemed clear to me that those whose hands were on the planchette were unwittingly guiding it.

The planchette provided clues suggesting that I might be right. When Bob asked if his favorite TV show was going to be renewed, the spirits adopted his spelling when they replied, "Probly." When Ann asked if I had a crush on her, the spirits said *yes* when she and her friend worked the planchette, and *no* when one of my friends and I worked it. And when we blindfolded our friends before turning them loose with the planchette, the spirits showed their resentment by spelling out gibberish.

None of my skepticism prevented me from thoroughly enjoying the Ouija board. It was a great toy. I even mentioned it to my grandmother, a 70-year-old German immigrant who spoke grammatically excellent English with a charming accent. She was to this teenager a refuge from things going not terribly well at home. I'd walk to her house, we'd have breakfast, I'd play piano for her, and then we'd listen to my records. She liked Chicago, and Jim Morrison's voice made her swoon.

When I told her about the Ouija board, she was intrigued. "Vell," she said, "let's go to za store und buy vun of zees veejee boards."

Ouija Board
(Photo: Bryan Bonner)

The store had an ample supply, so ve bought vun und brought it home. It did not disappoint. The planchette burst into action, facilely fielding one question after another. But things got interesting when Grandmother asked, "Ven vill Peter come home?"

The Ouija board replied, "In a few weeks."

I am the youngest of four boys. Pete, the second-youngest, was three years older than I and the one to whom I felt closest. The law had a nasty habit of frowning upon a few of his preferred activities, culminating in his being given a choice, at age 17, between jail and enlistment in the U.S. Armed Forces. Pete chose enlistment. He had been in the United States Navy not quite a year when Grandmother and I convened our interview with the spirits. It was not surprising that Grandmother would ask about him. Her passion for Jim Morrison took a back seat only to her passion for worrying, especially about her grandchildren.

Grandmother's follow-up question was, "How can zat be?"

Not one to mince words, the planchette replied, "He quit."

Yeah, like you can quit the Navy.

Neither of us took it seriously. I come from a long line of scoffers and unbelievers. Of these, Grandmother was one of the staunchest.

If the planchette took offense at our doubt, it bore the insult with silent grace. Perhaps that was because it knew it would have the last laugh.

A few weeks later I was home alone when the phone rang. It was a collect call from Naval Base San Diego. I accepted the charges. It was Pete. "I've been given an honorable discharge," he said. "I'll be home in three days."

The Ouija board was right.

Soon after Pete returned home, I told him about the Ouija board's prediction. It terrified him, and he gave me a stern warning to stay away from Ouija boards. When I shrugged it off, he grew ardent. "Once when some of my friends were using a Ouija board," he persisted, *they saw a blue lady walk out of a mirror.*"

I didn't buy Pete's blue lady any more than the idea of spirits guiding the planchette. Then as now, I chalked up the successful prediction to the fact that with millions of questions put to Ouija boards and other fortune-telling devices, it is inevitable that now and then an answer will pan out. If you happen to be present on one of those occasions, and not present for the millions of other, failed predictions, you may find yourself amazed.

S. Von Cyburg (a pseudonym) is a second-generation American. His grandparents left Germany for the United States shortly before the outbreak of World War II. His grandfather, a gifted engineer who worked on the Manhattan Project, arrived first and entered the country illegally. Von Cyburg calls himself an "author for hire," though he isn't quite sure what that means. "Cyburg" is pronounced KEY-burg. He's picky about that.

The Cat Came Back

Kenneth L. Feder

A journalist might say that I am "burying the lede" by beginning this story informing you that more than fourteen years after his death, Randolph remains one of the best friends I ever had. You see, what I left out is probably the most important part of my story: Randolph was not a human being. He was a cat. But *what* a cat.

Sure, he was a big, beautiful, orange tabby but he lacked pedigree or papers. He was, essentially, just an ordinary house cat. Except he wasn't ordinary. Not to me. Randolph was an incredibly intelligent and intensely social creature who truly was my good friend. The first cat with whom I shared my life, he belied the libel that domesticated felines are solitary beings and incapable of forming strong bonds with people. Randolph was all about making and maintaining those bonds with anyone who entered my house.

It made no difference if you were well known to him or a complete stranger. Sit at the kitchen table and he would join you. He wouldn't demand attention and he would always wait for the human to make the first move. There was no obsequious rubbing of his head against your hand begging for petting, no body swipe against your leg leaving a trail of fur and scent. He simply would closely watch whatever you were doing, acting as a kind of feline anthropologist intensely studying human behavior. But say one word to him, just one tiny indication that you welcomed his presence and invited interaction, and the damn cat would start purring. Furiously. I called him the "insta-purr kitty." You didn't have to pet him or scratch his ear, although those gestures were greatly appreciated. Generally, one kind word was all it took to get his motor running. He would respond to that one word, sit, gaze into your eyes with apparent devotion, and purr, apparently happy to merely be in the moment with you.

Occasionally, I have been accused of anthropomorphizing when I share tales of Randolph's great intelligence—about how he figured out the best way to use his haunches to effectively secure scratching posts that our other cats would invariably pull down on themselves. His ability to open any closed door, much to the embarrassment of visitors to our house who needed to use the bathroom. And how he would alert us when our kids were babies and were fussing in their cribs. In truth, as a long time college prof, I think it is more reasonable to accuse me of the dreaded "a" word—anthropomorphizing—when I ascribe human intelligence and complex emotions to many of the undergraduate students in my introductory courses than it is to apply it to my discussion of Randolph's abilities and personality.

As a writer of books, I spend a lot of time sequestered in my home office staring at a computer screen. Writing is a solitary, lonely task, yet when I wrote I was never alone. Randolph was my constant and welcome companion, usually just snoozing on my desk while I labored feverishly at the computer. Again, he didn't beg for or demand attention; he just craved human company.

Randolph
(Photo: Kenneth Feder)

His favorite "bed" was a pile of papers, usually representing a book chapter or two, resting just to the right of the computer screen and secured with a long rubber band. It was clear that the thing he liked most about those literary beds, in fact, were those rubber bands. For reasons not entirely clear to me, Randolph derived great enjoyment from hooking a sharp claw under the elastic and pulling it up until it slipped from his grasp, and snapped back onto the papers. No matter how many times he did it, he always seemed startled when it would snap back into place whereupon he would cock his head, looking for all the world like a scientist fascinated by an experimental result. And then he would do it again. And again. I admit that I sometimes found the repetitive "snaps" annoying, but if that was the price of his company, I was happy to pay it.

Randolph lived with us for nearly nineteen years. He died in December of 2002 after a brief bout with a ravaging cancer. Though we considered euthanasia toward the end, up until his last day he still ate heartily, used the litter box, and he could walk, however slowly. He clearly gave the impression that he wanted to stick around. Even the day before he died, he followed us from room to room, just as he always had, apparently insisting on being with another member of the pride, no matter how difficult it had become for him. In fact, on his final visit to the doctor, the vet told us he had never seen a cat as terminally ill as Randolph who could still function as well as he did. I remember quite clearly the vet telling us, "He sure seems to want to stick around as long as he can." We honored Randolph's wish. He left us on his own terms one chilly, early winter morning.

I was devastated, of course, but work is work and there were publishing deadlines and correspondence that wouldn't allow me to take time to grieve for the death of a pet. On the very afternoon of Randolph's death, in fact, I sat down in my home office and actually managed to get some writing done. The work was, if anything, therapeutic, although I was barely able to transcend the emptiness of the room without my good friend.

Okay, now here's where it gets weird. While typing away on the computer keyboard I heard a sharp, distinct crack from the pile of papers sitting to my right. The rubber band securing the pages had, for no discernible reason, sheared apart. It loudly snapped in two at just the moment when my grief for the loss of an otherwise nondescript orange cat was at its crescendo.

It was strange and disconcerting, I admit. And, of course, I recognized that it was merely a coincidence. Randolph's constant playing with similar rubber bands securing similar piles of papers had resulted in broken elastics several times previously. Okay, those breaks had always occurred while he was actually there playing with them, pulling at them and exceeding what a materials scientist would label their "elastic limit." It had never happened long after the fact. In all likelihood Randolph had pulled at the rubber band in question, perhaps multiple times before his death, rendering it significantly weakened and that's what caused it to break at that moment, without any additional feline encouragement. It was, of course, just a coincidence that it happened a few hours after he died, and while I was mourning the void in my life left by his death. Just a coincidence. Of course.

Or…and that's the problem for a skeptic. Or what? What other explanations can I plausibly offer? Did Randolph, up in kitty heaven where the bowls are always filled with Fancy Feast and there's catnip on every corner, sense my deep sorrow, get the OK from the Big Guy, and reach his mystical spirit paw down to my office to send me a sign that all is well? Seriously? Or did my own emotional turmoil trigger my hidden psychokinetic abilities, which paranormally plucked the elastic beyond its breaking point as a sort of final homage to my cat? Or hey, maybe the spirit of rubber bands felt my emotional pain and broke one of its own just to remind me of Randolph. Sure. Any of those make perfect sense. But, of course, they don't.

So I guess I'll have to be at least intellectually satisfied that it was all a coincidence because the other explanations, as comforting as any one of them (well, certainly the first one) would be, simply and sadly do not fit within any rational understanding of our world and the reality that defines our existence. As a skeptic I know and accept that. Randolph is gone, utterly, except as the sweet memory of a member of a different species, a kindred spirit who was, for nearly nineteen years, an esteemed and cherished member of the family.

As much as I might wish it, he isn't chasing mice and sitting on a cloud somewhere, watching over me and amusing himself with his own infinite collection of heavenly rubber bands. And, as a human being, I certainly can admit that acknowledging those cold facts doesn't make me happy. But the universe isn't in the business of making me happy. That, it turned out, became new kitty Aslan's job, which, I can report, he performed quite admirably, even though he showed no particular interest in pulling the rubber bands securing the chapter pages on which he also liked to snooze.

Dr. Kenneth Feder has a Ph.D. from the University of Connecticut. He has taught in the Department of Anthropology at Central Connecticut State University since 1977 where he is a full professor. His primary research interests include the archaeology of the native peoples of New England and the analysis of public perceptions about the human past. He is the author and co-author of *Frauds, Myths, and Mysteries: Science and Pseudoscience in Archaeology; The Past In Perspective: An Introduction to Human Prehistory,* and the *Encyclopedia of Dubious Archaeology*. His most recent project is *Ancient America: Fifty Archaeological Sites to See For Yourself.* The book is, effectively, a "time travel guide" for the archaeological tourist. He has been a talking head on several television documentaries about the human past. One producer has described him as being "a beacon of sanity in a sea of madness," about human antiquity, which actually is a very scary thought.

Time Out

David Fitzgerald

As a kid I had two mysterious experiences that I still can't explain.

When I was a young Southern Baptist kid growing up in Clovis, California, the church was our life. My family went to services twice on Sundays, and then again on Wednesday evenings. Sunday mornings we kids attended Sunday School class, followed by "Big Church," as we called it. Then we went back in the evening for another, slightly more informal service. Wednesdays we had choir practice. Except for attending elementary school, church was pretty much our entire social circle.

Clovis, California
(Photo: Clovis Chamber of Commerce)

This was the 1970s. Back then, it felt like a weird and insular time to be a Christian kid. To hear our preacher tell it, anybody outside our brand of born-again Christian was a hell-bound heathen. No one on TV or in the movies seemed to be displaying good Christian values, and it was the era of hippies and bikers and disco, women's libbers and liberals; except of course for a precious few courageous souls like Anita Bryant and the Reverend Billy Graham. The other kids in public school all seemed to be the wrong kind of believer: Catholic, Mormon, Jehovah's Witnesses, or stoners who *didn't even go to church at all.*

The decade was also a great time for the paranormal. The Bermuda Triangle, Bigfoot, UFOs, ESP, and Satanism (at least, according to Chick Tracts) were all the rage. "The X-Files" was still twenty-some years away, but we did have "Kolchak: the Night Stalker." During the 1970s all kinds of weirdness reigned; not least of all the fashion sense.

But Southern Baptists don't believe in *any of those things.* I mean, of course they believe in all kinds of goofy things, like the standard collection of Christian doctrine, talking snakes, Noah's Ark, the apostles speaking in tongues, and Jesus performing miracles, rising from the dead and ascending to heaven. They just don't put much stock in anything like that happening these days (at least, our particular brand didn't.)

So we'd roll our eyes when the Pentecostals handled venomous snakes, babbled in made-up sounding angelic languages or went into spasms while being filled with the Holy Spirit. We snickered at Catholic–style exorcisms with their silly holy water and Latin incantations. Everybody knew you just needed to be a born-again Christian to cast demons out in the name of Jesus! And we hated all those oily, cash-hungry TV evangelists who made all us Real Christians™ look bad. When it comes to all the other forms of Christianity, Southern Baptists can actually show some admirable skepticism.

I mention all this to let you know how tricky it could be to reconcile being an obedient Christian kid with being an enthusiastic sci-fi geek. It was a constant balancing act to find weird things to believe in that could still manage to fit inside the Baptist worldview. (Ghosts: No. The Loch Ness Monster: Yes!) And yet, I still had my own share of paranormal weirdness. I've had not one, but two strange experiences.

Oddly enough, they both occurred in the exact same spot, albeit years apart. Of course, they happened at church. To be exact, at the rusty old swing set that stood in a little yard tucked between our two main church buildings. In hindsight, that swing set was a rickety little deathtrap that would be right at home in some horror movie about creepy ghost children.

The first event happened one Wednesday evening, while my folks were at choir practice. I was stuck waiting for them, hanging out in our church's sad little play area with a few younger kids who were borderline toddlers and fairly useless company. It felt like I had been saddled with impromptu babysitting duty, so I was slightly resentful and pretty bored. It was getting late and dark enough that the stars were out. With little else to catch my attention, I happened to notice the flashing lights from two airplanes crossing the sky. Only… they *weren't* airplanes…

Looking closer, I saw they were more kite-shaped or spearhead-shaped, like a diamond on its side, and elongated on the bottom point. In fact, they looked like the Tholian ships in an old "Star Trek" episode. Their movement was eerily slow and fascinating. They were drifting towards each other, moving at a diagonal, even though they remained oriented horizontally. They drew closer and closer to one another, and I was afraid the two craft were going to collide.

At the very moment of impact, instead of an explosion, the two aircraft silently touched nose to nose, and moved off at different angles, never changing their slow, unearthly pace; bouncing away again like slow-motion billiard balls. Their trajectories seemed impossible for jets or planes. Both were now moving apart at reverse diagonals, although both kept their nose unwavering, perfectly level.

Wow! I just saw a UFO—a pair of them!

That was it. They didn't land, or emit a strange beam of light, or abduct me, or anything else. I spent a few quietly odd minutes watching this funny little aerial ballet moving across the night sky. Needless to say, nobody believed my story and before long I learned to stop talking about the experience.

But honestly, that's not the weird part. The truly bizarre thing is what happened later.

This was maybe a few years after the UFO sighting, or maybe it was only a few months later; I can't recall. It doesn't really matter. At any rate, it started out as some random Sunday evening, like any other.

The evening church service had just let out, and like the happy, newly-freed screaming kids we were, we proceeded to chase each other around outside, getting in a few precious minutes of kid's playtime before the grown-ups finished their chitchat and we all had to go home. We ran from the main sanctuary past the parking lot to a big field on the far side of the other two main church buildings, where the Sunday School classrooms and the all-purpose meeting room were. A bunch of us boys immediately ditched the girls and tore off back towards that same little grassy play area with the rattletrap swing set.

We were running through a little alleyway formed between two of the church buildings that led to the swing set area. It was a short throughway; maybe twenty feet long. There were four or five guys with me, all of us hooting and hollering. I was in the middle of the pack, barreling down at full speed with the rest of them. I remember seeing the backs of the boys just ahead of me, and hearing the sounds of the boys running behind me. I can still hear the clopping and the echoing of our tennis shoes as we pounded down the sideway.

When I reached the halfway point of the passageway, something strange happened.

I vaguely recall seeing a white flash. Then there was a sudden cessation of sound, like a freeze frame on the closing credits of a movie. Mostly, though, I remember a sensation that something *different* had occurred. All I really know for sure is that I ran out of the little passageway and suddenly *there was no one in front of me and there was no one behind me.*

I was alone.

Just a moment ago, we had gotten out of the evening service, with scads of kids running around, and grown-ups emerging from the church entrance and milling about out front. The parking lot was full. But now—just a moment later—all was silent. I stood there by the swing set, looking around and feeling utterly baffled. Then I walked over to the parking lot. The full parking lot was nearly empty; even *our* car was gone. All of them were *gone.*

I had never felt so confused in my life. I didn't even have time to imagine my friends were hiding or somebody was playing a joke on me. That was simply impossible. The sky had darkened to indigo, the moon was brightening and there was no one around anywhere.

I was alone.

Oddly, I don't remember being terrified that the Rapture had hit. Of course, after we all saw the movie *Thief in the Night* at a youth rally, the fear of being "left behind" to face the Antichrist and his evil minions haunted Christian kids of my generation anytime we couldn't find anyone at home when we expected. This wasn't like that. I wasn't scared. I was mystified.

I walked back to the main doors of the church. There was still a knot of stragglers near the entrance. Our pastor and his family were locking up the building for the night. One of his grandkids saw me and shouted, "David Fitzgerald! Your folks are looking for you! They went to the Brewers' house!" The Brewers were a family that went to our church; they lived a few blocks away.

If you had asked me how much time had elapsed from the time we all ran out of the church service to go play and the moment I heard this, my guess would have been two, maybe three minutes, if that. Five minutes tops. Now it appeared as though a whole hour of my life (or longer) had vanished in a single instant.

In hindsight, I wish I had thought to ask somebody what time it was right then. Oh well, everybody knows how to save the ship after it's sunk. I didn't even bother trying to talk to anybody there about my incident. I set off walking across the big grassy field that separated the Brewer's street from the church property, wondering all the while what had happened, and how on earth I would explain to my parents where I had been.

Sure enough, my family was at our friends' house. When I arrived my brothers and sister were playing out front with the Brewers' kids. My folks were very miffed at my unexplained disappearance, and my attempts at an explanation were unsuccessful. I was filled with that righteous childhood indignation that comes from having your marvelous experiences dismissed and getting in trouble for something *that wasn't even my fault.* Being a Baptist, I didn't even have any good swear words to vent my frustration.

To make matters even more bizarre, when I spoke to my church friends the next week, nobody remembered anything odd about that night at all. They remembered us all playing after church, but nothing about me disappearing for an hour. Sheesh! (That's about as salty as my language could get during the 1970s.)

To this day, I can remember both experiences vividly. I can see those two odd spearhead shapes and the uncanny grace with which they oh–so–slowly slid across the night sky. And yet in good skeptical 20/20 hindsight, I don't have any problem dismissing even my own UFO "sighting" as probably an optical illusion combined with wishful thinking and a fervent imagination. Looking back, I find it particularly suspicious that even now in my memory they looked like the spaceships from a classic "Star Trek" episode.

I've lived long enough and read enough about human psychology to know that our brains have more than enough ways to fool us and distort our memories. At the end of the day, we're story-telling animals with a love of mystery. We take joy in crafting a thrilling narrative, even if we're the only one in the audience. And while I'm driven to explore the universe and find answers to its vast secrets, there are some mysteries I'm okay with not figuring out.

Which may be a good thing in this case, since I have no better explanation for that missing hour, or what really happened to me for that lost span of time.

David Fitzgerald is the author of *NAILED* and *The Complete Heretic's Guide to Western Religion* series. (Secretly, he is also an erotica writer under the name Kilt Kilpatrick.) He lectures internationally at universities, churches and national secular events. David lives in San Francisco with his wife: Writer, producer and movie actress Dana Fredsti. They are at work on a new science-fiction trilogy coming out soon from Titan Books. www.facebook.com/david.fitzgerald.33633

If The Spirit Moves You

Chris French

As a psychologist, I am well aware of the unreliability of eyewitness testimony. Memory does not work like a video camera. Instead, we typically remember the gist of what happened but forget the details. Entire events, no matter how significant, can be lost, distorted, or even unintentionally fabricated by our minds.

Knowing this, I took the precaution of getting some of the other people who were involved in the tale that I am about to tell to read it over before I submitted it. That proved to be an interesting exercise in itself, as I shall later relate. The version you are about to read first is the way I remember this strange episode four decades later.

I didn't travel abroad until I was 22 years old. So you would think that I would at least remember where it was that I went, right? I know it was to Austria but I couldn't recall exactly where. I asked a couple of the people I had gone with—and got two different answers. One of them rang more of a bell than the other: The town of Nassereith. I had gone there with a group of seven friends from university.

At the hotel, there were double rooms and single rooms. Naturally, we all wanted a single room. I don't remember how we decided who would be the lucky individuals who got the single rooms but I have a vague recollection that we played a series of (probably quite silly) games to select the winners. However we did it, I was a winner. Lucky me (or so I thought.)

One of our habits as students, to keep ourselves amused in the evenings (after a few pints of beer at the local pub), was to have a Ouija board session. We were all poor so we didn't own one of those posh commercially available boards with a fancy planchette. We couldn't afford to waste money that could otherwise be exchanged for beer. So instead we made a homemade version. We wrote the letters of the alphabet on scraps of paper along with the digits from one to ten and arranged them in a circle on a smooth table. We then took a wineglass and passed it around the group, each member breathing into it before placing the upturned glass in the center of the circle. Finally, each placing a single finger on the glass, one of us would ask the question, "Is anybody there?" After a while, the glass would appear to move, somewhat hesitantly, of its own volition (albeit with fingers always still in contact) to the letter "Y" then "E" and then "S." Further questions would be asked and usually the movement of the glass became faster and smoother.

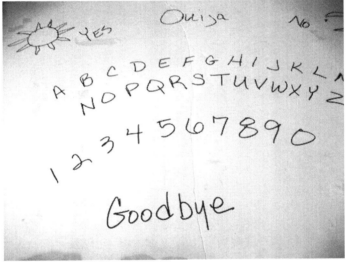

Homemade Ouija Board
(Photo: Munro House)

This procedure has long been believed by some to be a method of spirit communication. When we did it as students, none of us really believed spirits were moving the glass. (Actually, there was one of our group of housemates who *did* believe this—but he scuttled off to his bedroom the moment anyone suggested a Ouija session and steadfastly refused to take part.) Even so, I do not think that at that stage of my life I fully understood what was going on. It wasn't until a few years later that I became skeptical of paranormal claims (thanks to reading James Alcock's wonderful book, *Parapsychology: Science or magic?*)

As anyone who has ever taken part in a Ouija session can testify, it certainly feels as though the glass is either moving of its own volition or else being pushed by an external force. Of course, it is always possible that one or more of the other members of the group may be intentionally pushing the glass around but you feel absolutely certain that *you* are not doing so. As the session progressed, different members of the group would take their finger off the glass and just watch the glass moving around in response to questions, as if to prove that they were certainly not the one moving it.

So, there we were in Austria and we decided one evening, no doubt after having consumed considerable amounts of alcohol, that it would be fun to have a session with a Ouija board. As usual, the one member of our group who took the idea of spirits seriously scuttled off to his room and the rest of us settled down for what we hoped would be an amusing hour or two. We had been noticing that the success of these sessions appeared to depend to some extent on who took on the main role of asking the questions. For us, that person was Andy, a down-to-earth Yorkshire lad. If you met Andy and spoke to him, you would probably get the impression that he had all of the mediumistic ability of a teapot. But he did seem to get the best results.

But this time, even with Andy asking the questions, not much was happening. For a long time the glass hardly moved at all, and we were about to end the session when suddenly the glass started to move slowly towards the letter "J" then "E" and followed by "W." None of us were Jewish but I suspect, possibly as a result of being on the European continent, that all of our minds turned to a dark and terrible period of world history. Then the glass spelled out the word, "AUSCHWITZ." This was definitely *not* the fun-filled Ouija board session we had been anticipating so we immediately stopped playing. At that moment, tears streamed down Andy's face. We all saw them. Andy said he felt no emotion whatsoever—but we all saw those tears.

By now, we were all a bit freaked out. I was still feeling a bit shaken when I went to bed. The joy I had felt at the prospect of having a room to myself was gone. I'm not sure what I thought I had just witnessed but whatever it was, I didn't like it. I didn't like it at all. Even with my bedside light on, I took a long time to get to sleep. Eventually I did drift off, only to awaken to see Rob, one of my other travel companions, sitting on my floor with his back against the wall. What the hell was Rob doing in my room? I looked again. It wasn't Rob at all. It was just the way my clothes were hanging on a chair. That was it though, I'd had enough. Like a frightened child, I snuck into Andy and Rob's room and spent the rest of the night with them.

So, what did I make of that strange night all of these years later, having written books and articles on the psychology of anomalous experiences?

Seeing Rob in my room when he wasn't really there was a simple case of pareidolia. As defined in Robert Todd Carroll's *Skeptic's Dictionary*, pareidolia is, "a type of illusion or misperception involving a vague or obscure stimulus being perceived as something clear and distinct." Common examples of pareidolia include seeing faces in clouds or in the grain of wood or in stains on a floor. In my case, the outline of my clothes on the chair looked vaguely like a person and my confused brain, having just awoken from an uneasy sleep, did the rest.

The movement of the glass during the Ouija board sessions is best explained as being a manifestation of the ideomotor effect, a term first coined by William Benjamin Carpenter in 1852. Again, the *Skeptic's Dictionary* provides a concise definition: "The influence of suggestion or expectation on involuntary and unconscious motor behavior." In other words, yes, we really were pushing the glass around the table but without being consciously aware that we were doing so.

So it appears that there are perfectly normal non-paranormal explanations for both the movement of the wineglass and the unexpected appearance of Rob in my bedroom. The only thing not yet explained are the tears that ran down Andy's face—and that is the detail that took on more significance when I checked the accuracy of my account with my other travel mates. Andy's memory of the events in question was very much in agreement with my own, except, amazingly, Andy had no recollection whatsoever of tears during a Ouija session. Others there remembered an incident where tears ran down Andy's cheeks during a Ouija session—but were unsure whether it happened in Austria or on a different occasion.

On reflection, I wonder if I ever witnessed Andy's inexplicable tears at all. Perhaps that happened on an occasion when I was not actually present and I just pictured it in my head, and later mistook my imagined memory with a witnessed memory? Did I then unintentionally weave that false memory into the Austrian events? I simply don't know. But I feel it did really happen some time, somewhere.

In fact, now I think about, did I really see my "apparition" of Rob on the same night as the other incidents? Maybe not. I am reasonably sure that I did indeed have that experience but maybe it was on a different night?

We have known since the classic work on memory by Sir Frederic Bartlett back in the 1930s that the accounts given in stories become changed and distorted in the retelling, typically in the direction of "improving" the tale. So maybe I unintentionally combined three separate incidents into one story, one that I have recounted as an honest recollection of events on numerous occasions when the conversation has turned to Ouija boards and other spooky phenomena. I guess we should all be just a little cautious in assuming that stories told around the campfire are 100% to be believed.

Professor Chris French is Head of the Anomalistic Psychology Research Unit in the Psychology Department at Goldsmiths, University of London. He has published over 150 articles and chapters covering a wide range of topics within psychology. His main area of research is the psychology of paranormal beliefs and anomalous experiences. His most recent books are *Anomalistic Psychology*, co-authored with Nicola Holt, Christine Simmonds-Moore, and David Luke, and *Anomalistic Psychology: Exploring Paranormal Belief and Experience*, co-authored with Anna Stone.

My Incubus

Sheldon W. Helms

Back in the 1980s, I found myself caught up in New Age spirituality, along with millions of others. This was the second wave of the New Age movement—led by Shirley MacLaine, if only by proxy. I spent the better part of that decade regularly visiting my local New Age bookstore, where I purchased all manner of spiritual accouterments, including books, crystals, blessed candles, and psychic readings.

One day, during an I Ching reading, the reader suggested that I might benefit from more meditation. She was shocked to learn that I didn't meditate at all. In fact, I knew nothing about it. This conversation culminated in my purchase of the book *How to Meditate*, and also led to my first personal experience with the paranormal.

The instructions in this book seemed simple enough, but I soon found them difficult to employ. Sitting comfortably and closing my eyes was easy, but every attempt I made to "clear my mind" was met with some sort of outside distraction. Eventually, I began performing my meditations at night, just before bed. Once everyone else in the house was asleep, I'd sit on my bedroom floor and follow the instructions to the letter. My mind calmed, I would make my hour long foray into "mindfulness," thinking of nothing—which is harder than it sounds—and listening only to my own natural breathing pattern. I really did feel better after a few weeks of meditation, and of course, I associated every bit of good fortune or other pleasantry with the fact that I was now "in tune with the Universe."

About three weeks into this new habit, something strange began to happen. As I sat there on the floor, concentrating on thinking about nothing, I'd sometimes find myself leaving my body and entering the room in a non-corporeal state. In other words, I began to Spirit Walk, or astral-project, or whatever you want to call it. I didn't mean to do this; it just happened. The first time, it lasted only for a few brief moments. As soon as I realized what was going on, I would immediately return to my body and open my eyes again, my heart racing. I have to admit, I thought it was rather funny. It didn't frighten me at all. In fact, I didn't even think of it as something real or otherworldly. For some reason, I thought of it as hallucinatory, a sort of game that my unruly mind was playing with me as I attempted to master this meditation thing.

As time went on, I not only became better at meditating, but my out-of-body experiences became more frequent and much more realistic. I still couldn't command them to happen, but once they did, I could pretty much control where I went and what I did. I could walk over to the closet and peer inside. And I could turn and look at my bed, or observe the bindings of the books sitting on my bookshelf. I couldn't move anything or pick up an object, but I could move my body about just fine and observe. On one occasion, I remember looking directly at myself and thinking, "Wow. I really need to get my hair cut." None of this seemed particularly real to me though, and I'm still not sure why that was. Today, my skeptical mind tells me that I already knew very well what my room looked like and what was in it, and it would be quite easy for my brain to pull from that knowledge and recreate it all for me. And I'd certainly spent enough time looking in the mirror to know that I needed a haircut. So, although these experiences were nothing like dreams because they were much more realistic and detailed, I also didn't fully accept them as real, giving me a license to have fun with them and laugh them off.

One evening, about a month into my training, all of that changed.

That night's meditation started as all the others. I lit an incense stick, turned off most of the lights in the room, sat cross-legged on the floor in the corner, assumed the Lotus position, closed my eyes, and began concentrating on my breathing. Within moments I was suddenly in my non-corporeal form, sitting on the edge of my bed. This shocked me because I hadn't walked over there as I usually did when leaving my real body; I just suddenly found myself sitting on the bed. Adding to my horror, I suddenly realized that I couldn't move! I knew that my "real" body was over in the corner, and I could still smell the sandalwood incense filling the room, but my "body" refused to take any commands whatsoever. I did my best to avoid panicking, but I had never been so terrified!

(Photo: Astro Ulagam)

With my head facing the open closet in front of me, I simply sat and stared, looking out of the corners of my eyes to take in as much of my surroundings as possible. It was then that I suddenly became aware of a presence to my right. I never actually saw it, but I could somehow tell that it was a sort of blackness; small, dark, and warm, it was sitting beside me on the bed, looking at me. And it was evil. Pure, unadulterated evil and malice emanated from this entity to my right, and I wanted nothing more than to get as far away from it as possible.

I could feel my heart pounding inside my chest, and I could feel my face flush. But my body still remained frozen, my panic rising. As I look back on the experience, I realize that a strange duality existed in this experience. I didn't think of my non-corporeal existence as being real, but somehow I interpreted this entity as being quite real and quite dangerous. The fact that those are contradictory notions didn't occur to me then, but I doubt they would have mattered at the time. I was positively consumed with a desperate, terrifying need to get out of that room. Yet, I was trapped!

It's hard to say exactly how long this scene lasted, but just as I began to give in to my fate and realize that I was completely at the mercy of the evil thing next to me, I heard it give a little chuckle, and suddenly vanish. I never saw it, so I couldn't have seen it disappear, but I knew that it was no longer there. I was instantly relieved, but found that my "body" still refused all commands to move. Moments later, I awoke in my actual body, covered in sweat and leaning against the wall behind me.

I got up and turned on all the lights, looking around the room for signs of an intruder or…anything! But all was just as I had left it. My sense of time would be somewhat distorted when meditating, so I couldn't help but wonder how long this ordeal had gone on. Somewhat annoyed at myself for not glancing at the wall clock before I'd started, I then remembered the incense I had lit before my meditation began. The length of the stick might give me some time estimate, since the ones I bought lasted about 30 minutes. Picking up the still-burning stick, I was shocked to find very little had turned to ash. Hazarding a guess, I estimated that the entire life-altering trial had lasted no more than 5 minutes. But those five minutes had seemed like an hour in hell.

My days as an amateur meditator were over. I was convinced that I'd managed to somehow invite an interloper from an evil dimension into my home. I worried that any future attempt to meditate might bring it back, or worse, take me into whatever terrible realm it came from. I threw away the meditation book immediately, eschewed any invitations to meditate at friends' readings or spiritual gatherings, and still find myself embarrassingly uncomfortable when I smell sandalwood incense.

Of course, my interpretation of that night is quite different these days. Not long after this experience, I took my first psychology course and fell in love with the subject. After that, I took many more such courses, eventually earning degrees in psychology and education. Over time, I came to understand that scholars who study sleep have much more convincing—not to mention, realistic—explanations for what I experienced.

As it turns out, it's common for people to hallucinate when entering a sleep state from wakefulness. These are called hypnagogic hallucinations. Some studies even show that meditation can trigger such states in otherwise healthy people. But I think it's more likely that I simply fell asleep while attempting to meditate. Many who have such an experience also suffer sleep paralysis, finding themselves at least partially conscious, but still experiencing the shut-down from our cortex to our peripheral nerves that prevents us from acting out our dreams. Thus, far from being evidence of the supernatural, my horrifying meditation was a textbook example of the sort of hypnagogic episodes that people have experienced, perhaps as long as there have been humans.

The first report of a hypnagogic hallucination was made in 1664 by the Dutch physician Isbrand Van Diemerbroeck (1609-1674), which he published in a collection of case histories. Entitled "*Of the Night-Mare*," it details the nightly experiences of a 50-year-old woman, and aside from my attempts to learn how to meditate, this read like a description of what happened to me. This poor woman's hallucinations also included a dark form, or Incubus, in her case laying on top of her and making it difficult for her to breathe.

Why my little demon sat beside me, apparently mocking my inability to escape, is open to interpretation and speculation.

Sheldon W. Helms is a professor of psychology at Ohlone College where he runs a speaker series hosting top-name scientists, skeptics, and authors from around the world. He serves as a board member of the Bay Area Skeptics, and on the planning committee for SkeptiCal, the Bay Area's conference on science and skepticism. Sheldon has written for the James Randi Educational Foundation, and regularly gives public science talks on a variety of topics related to the science of psychology. He hosts the podcast ShelShocked.

They Held Their Applause Until The End

George Hrab

There are no such things as ghosts.

Well, the possibility that ghosts exist is really unlikely, if you just think about it logically for a second. Apart from everyone alive right now, everyone else who's ever lived is now dead. So, if even the tiniest fraction of the deceased could come back to haunt those not quite dead yet, we should all be inundated with spooks, specters, phantasms, ghosts, ghouls, and Marilyn Monroe. You should not be able to throw an empty Stay-Puft Marshmallow bag into your trash can without accidentally hitting a ghost. Or a dozen.

Right?

Estimates say that there are about one hundred billion dead humans. Let's say that only one in a million deceased persons can appear as a ghost on a daily basis (tough union.) With that completely arbitrary rule, there should be one hundred thousand ghost sightings per day. You know what does happen one hundred thousand times a day? Lightning strikes. The earth is hit daily by about one hundred thousand bolts of lightning. Yes indeed. With our "one in a million dead people get to be apparitions" rule, ghosts should be as common as freaking lightning. I went to YouTube and typed in "lightning strike." There are 584,000 results. Not all of these are real of course, but if you figure that getting excellent footage of an unpredictable flash of light lasting less than a second can be managed hundreds of thousands of times, filming a ghost (who one could assume would at least occasionally want to stick around for longer than a burst of lightning) should be as common as footage of guys spectacularly destroying their nads via missed skate board tricks. (282,000 results.)

So, from a purely statistical standpoint, the existence of ghosts is very hard to justify—let alone all of the philosophical, religious, logical, and temporal questions raised by the topic.

All that being said, just about everyone (alive or dead I'm sure) has probably had at least one experience that has defied logic and reason while causing seconds of taint-puckering fear, befuddlement and apprehension.

Here then, is a story about my mysterious experience.

After getting my degree and graduating from Moravian College in Bethlehem, Pennsylvania, I somehow managed to convince the Music Department to hire me as a music librarian. This process involved some begging, sight-singing Schubert lieder, sugar cake, and a few hand puppets. (Moravians are a curious bunch.) Having this job meant that not only was I in charge of the music library, but I was required to attend and record every concert that took place on campus in order to maintain and update the department's performance archive. That meant that I had keys to EVERYWHERE. This was pretty cool. All the more so because the building that houses the Moravian Music Department, the Brethren's House, is one of the oldest in Pennsylvania, having been built in 1748. Yes indeed: I had total access to a structure that is twenty-eight years older than the country it's in. Working in a building like this was quite interesting, primarily because after-hours, once all the students have left and the sun has set, IT IS CREEPY AS FUCK.

Peter Hall
(Photo: George Hrab)

My skepticism and rationality were pretty well in place by this point of my life, so I used to revel in the fact that the hairs on the back of my neck would prick up as I walked through a darkened two-hundred-plus-year-old hallway at midnight. I would tell myself that ghosts were logically impossible and that what I was experiencing was a normal mammalian response to an unsure and mildly stressful situation. I loved that I could ride the fear and use my (youthfully-bravado induced) rationality as a type of shield from being completely frightened. I used to make it a point to go up late at night to the dreaded and un-finished "fourth floor," which was used as storage for dusty old mirrors, broken harpsichords, rocking chairs, and un-tenured bassoon teachers. It was eerie as hell—with every creak and squeak and moan of a floorboard inciting my reptilian brain to implore that my legs flee and take me elsewhere.

It's with a certain irony then that the coldest, most pancreatic-pounding scare I ever had in this venerable music facility happened during a beautifully bright and shiny morning…

It was around 11:00 a.m. one sunny Sunday that I found myself in the building with the task of getting my recording equipment cleaned up from the previous night's concert. I had decided to leave it all set up, knowing that I could return the following day and put it all away without the hassle of making my late night even later. On that next morning, in order to get to the concert hall on the far side of the arts campus, I would have to walk through three separate buildings: the Brethren's House is attached onto Peter Hall, a late 19th century brick addition, which then feeds into Foy Hall, the modern portion of the facility that was built in the 1980s. All of these buildings are interconnected with modified hallways and stairs. The entire structure sits on a significant slope, so in order to get from The Brethren's House to Foy Hall, you have a choice of floors from which to make your trip and you have to either walk under or through Peter Hall.

I decided to walk through Peter Hall because I was on the appropriate floor. As I approached the door and was about to open it, I heard rapturous applause and realized that there was a concert in progress. There were a number of organizations that often used this space for private performances, including church-related activities and local music student programs. These were not college-sponsored events, but were simply room rentals, so I often wouldn't know the schedule of these concerts, especially on a Sunday morning.

I was relieved that I had heard the clapping and stopped myself when I did, because the set of doors I was about to open were located just to the side and front of the audience, insuring there was no way I could subtly hide the fact that they were opened. There was even a common embarrassing ritual wherein a person trying to walk through the building would boldly swing open the entrance to Peter Hall, not realizing that a concert was taking place. Red-faced and horrified under the judgmental glare of one hundred and fifty turned heads, they would self-consciously close the door. I was glad that I had narrowly avoided this Jerry Lewisian scenario, and re-directed my route downstairs to use the hallway that ran one floor lower and under Peter Hall.

I worked my way to Foy Hall, retrieved my equipment, and then walked briskly back to the Brethren's House to store all of my gear. I decided to go back to the level on which Peter Hall was located (but now from the opposite side) to grab a soda from a vending machine there. As I approached the machine, I saw that the doors to the south side entrance of Peter Hall were propped open. I was curious as to why the doors at this entrance would be open during a concert, and decided that I should gently shut them to prevent any potential disruption from this side of the facility. As I approached the entry and glanced into the space, my face had an involuntary reaction that mainly consisted of it instantly deciding to cosplay Edvard Munch's "The Scream."

Why?

Well… There was no one in the room.

It was completely empty.

Peter Hall
(Photo: George Hrab)

I had distinctly heard a hundred people applauding just moments before. I had heard their clapping so clearly that I had changed my route. Here I was just minutes later, on the opposite side of the room, and there was absolutely no one in it. My entire round trip had taken less than five minutes, so there was no way that an entire room of concert attendees could have filed out that quickly. And even if they had, at least there would have been organizers or someone cleaning up and re-setting the stage.

The room lights weren't even on.

As I stood in the doorway aghast, the hairs on my arms and the back of my neck instantly decided to form a conga line. My hands started shaking and my stomach pretended that the night before had been my bachelor party. I felt confused and ill, and was the most freaked-out I had ever been on a Sunday morning since first counting communion partakers as a ten-year-old Catholic altar boy.

My rational mind knew that I was mistaken and had just misheard, but the part of my brain that has a little chin-beard like Shaggy's wasn't having it. Zoinks indeed. To this day, I still have no real explanation. I worked in that department for another two years and never experienced anything remotely close to what happened that Sunday morning. I listened to pipe sounds, trains passing by, gas leaks, water flushing, baritones gargling, sophomores arguing and various other sonic anomalies that might have explained the incident, but I never again heard anything resembling that phantom applause.

There are a slew of websites and books and television shows devoted to talking about "haunted" sites in Bethlehem, PA—many of which talk about Moravian College's arts campus. They all speak of late-night hauntings, darkened corridors, and midnight apparitions... but to me, being scared in the dark is way too easy. Make someone shit themselves at 11:00 a.m. and then you've really got something.

Multi-instrumentalist, singer, songwriter, producer, composer, and heliocentrist George Hrab has written and produced six independent CDs and a concert DVD; published two books; recorded hundreds of episodes of an award-winning podcast; emceed countless science conferences; been a TEDx speaker; and has even performed for former President Bill Clinton. He's traveled to four continents promoting critical thinking, science, and skepticism through story and song. George is considered one of the preeminent skeptic/science/atheist/geek-culture music icons currently living in his apartment. www.georgehrab.com

A Tourist On Another Plane

Deborah Hyde

The working hours had been brutal. But when you're healthy, you can work that much—you really can. Your mind and your desire push you through. The weakness waits until you've finished.

Usually.

I had been working on a movie, making (among many other things) a costume for a horse. On the film-set at 3am in the middle of a chilly night, the ungrateful creature in its couture ensemble glared at me balefully as I stifled my cough yet again, trying not to spoil the sound on the take.

They were setting fire to a small forest that night and I could have stayed—just for the spectacle—but I was too tired to care. And anyway, my chest and throat hurt too much, so I went home after the shoot.

I sleep on my back—it's like I'm modeling for my own tomb effigy, but with murmuring and thrashing. Anyone in the know will tell you that sleeping supine makes you a bad candidate for sleep paralysis.

Or a good candidate, if you're into that sort of thing. Hardly anybody is.

Surveys show that this harmless sleep 'blip' is experienced once or twice in a lifetime by many, and repeatedly by a few. Wakefulness, combined with a correct perception of your environment will lead you to conclude that you are conscious. And you are—kind of. The residual bodily paralysis of dreaming sleep (who wants to act out their dreams, after all?) and the intrusion of REM phenomena-like images and sounds make this state a strange hybrid. Add the almost habitual sense of deathly fear and you have the oddest of experiential cocktails.

You can get better at coping with sleep paralysis and, over the years, I have. If you're patient you can turn it into lucid dreaming although this requires a bit of dread-management.

I lay there—on my back—desperate to fall asleep. And then every time I sank into sleep, I'd cough. An EEG would have looked like seismograph output from an ominously rumbling Mount Etna. So close to sleep. Then: "Cough."

People who suffer from sleep paralysis will tell you that it may be accompanied by disturbances in the sensation of their body's relationship to the world. They may feel like they are floating, flying and falling. Also, the feeling of being dragged out of bed. Not tonight, but regularly enough for it to be familiar.

"Cough."

When I was a child, my mother taught me how to induce a feeling of floating as I was falling sleep. She and my father were always patient when I had terrifying nightmares and, once, the absolute conviction that there was a poltergeist in the room.

She had died over a year ago. It's a shame—she would have liked the horse costume.

"Cough."

What about that poltergeist thing? I awoke in a dark room and heard a sound like pebbles being tossed up in the air and caught in a palm. But the phantom hand grew tired of its absent-minded juggling; it threw the pebbles against my bedroom radiator. I had never heard anything so certainly in all my life. *I had heard it.* The next day revealed an exotic Norwegian coin that had been stuck to the wall with a strip of tape, had finally succumbed to gravity in the small hours. The tape, gradually unpeeling from its backing paper, had sounded like pebbles being tossed up and down. The coin's eventual collision with the radiator below combined with my brain's desire to perceive a story with an actor—an intelligence, an agent—had provided the rest.

"Cough."

If you're prone to sleep paralysis, you can discourage it by practicing good sleep hygiene: Don't do anything that will make you plunge right into REM sleep—like getting over-tired or sleeping weird hours; and don't sleep on your back.

No cough. Deep rest and relaxation. Closed eyes. Calm.

I felt a massive "whoosh" as I was pulled out of my body through my feet and then stood upright just as violently. I looked down to see myself lying on my back. And there, to one side of the bed, was my mother.

We hugged, and I asked her how she was. She was fine. Then a discomforting thought struck me and my spectral brow furrowed.

"But am *I* alright?" I ask as I look, a little distressed, at my supine form. I knew I had been ill, but I didn't think it was *that* bad.

She laughed: "You're fine."

Cool. So we walked out of the bedroom and soon the environment morphed into something else.

This hadn't been my first out-of-body-experience (OBE), nor would it be my last. But it was always good to see my mother. I really think I suffered less grief than the rest of my family for having these lifelike experiences.

These OBEs are so realistic that there are times I tread gingerly through a dream location in case I really am walking using my real body, and am just hallucinating a floor where there are actually stairs.

Our world is created by our brains: During consciousness and during altered consciousness, as in dreams. Anyone who has experienced lucid dreaming or OBEs will tell you they are hyper-real, a super-detailed version of the mundane. I've often looked around in lucidity to analyze whether there's as much detailed information there as I later remember. There is.

I feel the rocket-fuel of my lucidity being drained by the hi-octane suck of the experience. Whichever chemicals the brain uses for this, they are limited, and I can sense them dwindling. Regular experiencers know how to prolong it: A vestibular disturbance like spinning on the spot does it for some; a kinesthetic sensation, like rubbing my hands together does it for me. Then my brain injects some more juice into the neuro-engine for just a little longer.

The chemistry of these experiences is somewhat understood. It is proposed that many people have vivid dreams but lack the memory and the concentration to recall and manipulate them. If you want assistance, there are supplements you can take. But beware of chemicals bought from the Internet; in my experience you need the mental discipline too, to avoid getting stuck in dark places. It's a bit like taking steroids: They only really help if you're already training hard.

Investigating neural correlates is a fascinating pastime, but we humans are concerned with meaning to the degree that we search for it—whether it's there or not. Sleep paralysis experiences, lucid dreaming, and OBEs are very profound experiences. Speaking personally, they're some of the most overwhelming I have ever had. But what if they're not the *point* of anything?

Have you ever heard of a spandrel? In architecture, a spandrel is a triangular area, described by a graceful curve, between the vertical and horizontal axes of a load-bearing arch. It's such a pleasing space that people usually decorate them with paintings and adornments. This artwork can command attention to the point that a spandrel appears to be the purpose of the structure.

**Spandrels on the Thomas Jefferson Building,
Washington, D.C.
(Photo: Encyclopedia Britannica)**

The concept of a spandrel can be expanded to explain how our intellectual sense of purpose—or even elegance and beauty—can misdirect our focus and cause us to infer wrong causal relationships. To use a biological metaphor, spandrels can be redefined as byproducts of adaptations that are not necessarily adaptive in themselves (although they can end up being so.)

So it's not about where you arrive, so much as the path by which you take to get there. Those elements that seem so subjectively important to us may play no part in the creation of the phenomenon at all and, ultimately therefore, have no importance.

All that we really have is the meaning we give to our relationships and experiences. If our pain and pleasure matter at all, then by whatever mechanism they arrive at our attention, they are surely worth contemplation.

Some people think that religion is a spandrel. I do. Some people think that lucid dreaming, hypnopompic and hypnogogic hallucinations, out-of-body experiences and near-death experiences are spandrels. I do. But that doesn't mean they're worthless or irrelevant.

Many people have an anomalistic experience and end up with a supernatural explanation. But I think that's a waste of an opportunity. I see several applications for these phenomena that are more useful than superstition or religion: One may be regarded as objective and scientific. The other is less so but, in my opinion, is every bit as valuable.

The first is that that we can often tell how things work when they don't work very well; those times that the seamless swish of stage-management stutters to reveal the mistimed mechanism underneath. The perfect coherence of mind and body wouldn't attract much attention unless it failed from time to time. Anomalous experiences of the types I have had are unusual, but quite similar in nature across experiencers, and that must tell us something about the way we perceive these experiences in our brains.

In fact, it seems that it does. Studies suggest that an area between the two lobes of the brain, the right temporoparietal junction, helps to integrate our bodies and our sense of self. Direct stimulation of the area provokes the kind of experiences that the rest of us have when we are sleep-deprived or ill. We have undoubtedly just started on this chapter of knowledge, and it will be fascinating to watch it unfold.

The second is, that as an insight onto your own psyche, these experiences can't be beaten. Whether you are seeking therapy, insight, impossible experiences (like walking through walls), grief counseling, the chance to develop mental discipline, or just a new perspective on life, these experiences can be as powerful—maybe more so—than traditional methods. I wouldn't trade my strange experiences for the world.

Deborah Hyde is editor of *The Skeptic* magazine, which has been published in the UK for over twenty-five years (www.skeptic.org.uk). She writes, speaks and broadcasts about religion, folklore, superstition and culture. www.DeborahHyde.com

The Merry Mystic:

My Life As A Palm Reader
Ray Hyman

For my seventh birthday, my father gave me some simple magic tricks. I practiced these tricks many times and then performed them for show-and-tell at my school. Apparently my teacher was impressed because she invited me to perform for the Parent Teacher's Association. So I did. And they paid me $5.00.

That was in 1935, and in those days, five dollars went a long way. I went to a local printer and spent some of that money having him make business cards for me. He designed a card with a drawing of a rabbit in a hat, and also gave me the title of "The Merry Mystic" (because our city was on the Mystic River.) I distributed these cards all over the city. Soon, I was performing magic shows for different groups and functions. I was convinced that I would become a professional magician.

After a few years of performing the same show I felt that I needed to add some new routines. So I added a memory act, a hypnosis act, and other novelties to my repertoire. By the time I was a teenager, I was no longer doing magic shows, as such. Instead, I was performing mentalism. I preferred doing straight magic, but I discovered that I got more bookings by advertising myself as a mentalist. And my clients were willing to pay more for this, too.

My mentalism show included reading minds, making predictions, influencing volunteers to do my bidding, and other seemingly psychic demonstrations. Every once in a while, I would give a "psychic" reading to a spectator. I quickly discovered that these cold readings were, by far, the most popular part of my act. Despite my efforts to create spectacular mentalism effects, to give the appearance of reading people's minds and predicting the future, and to influence and control people's decisions, my psychic readings were what really impressed my audiences.

By now I was sixteen and I decided to add a new act to my repertoire that would exploit people's strong interest in psychic readings. I considered a number of possible divination systems, including astrology, Tarot, and numerology. Astrology required drawing up complicated charts and I couldn't see how the planets and other celestial bodies could affect the personalities of individuals on Earth. Logically, Tarot and numerology just didn't seem like they could work either. I was about to give up on the idea when I discovered a book about palm reading.

This caught my attention because the hand is a part of the body. I read that some medical conditions could be diagnosed by features in the hand. And anthropologists had theorized that, because of our tool making skills, humans became the most intelligent and dominant animal on our planet. Maybe there was something to palmistry?

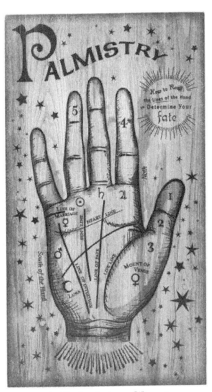

A Palmistry Chart
(Image: Scary Jerry)

I went to the library and borrowed every book they had on palm reading. I read about the interpretations of the lines on the palm, the shape of the palm, the relative length of the fingers as well as the phalanges, the size and resilience of the mounts, the meaning of the different patterns of fingerprints, the texture and color of the skin, the shape and markings on the fingernails, and the size of the knuckles. I learned as much as I could about palmistry and then announced that I was open for business.

I spent the next six years (1944–1950) working as a professional palm reader.

When I began this new venture, I didn't believe that palmistry was paranormal. I simply read a person's palm according to what I had learned from the palmistry books. It was no surprise that my clients accepted their readings as uniquely descriptive of themselves and their problems. As a skeptic, I was aware that palm readings contained vague statements and general descriptions that apply to everyone. But palmistry also provides tools for making very specific statements. Almost all palmistry texts provide guidelines for locating and dating concrete events that have happened or will happen. During a reading, I might notice a break in the client's heart line, which occurs at a location corresponding to thirty years of age. According to palmistry theory, this break indicates either a serious heart problem or an unfortunate break up of a romantic relationship. A break in the client's headline at approximately ten years of age could be interpreted concretely as damage to the head (such as a concussion) or as a psychological trauma. Such dating of concrete events can be done for each line on a person's hands.

I was astonished at how frequently my clients validated these concrete statements. I was convinced that such validations happened too frequently to be coincidental. As a result, I concluded that the markings on the hand truly pointed to actual events in the client's life. I took it as evidence for a connection between signs in the hand and the personality and intellectual qualities of the hand's owner.

I could provide many examples of how my belief in palm reading was validated by the reactions from my satisfied customers. I can't recall a single client who had any doubts about the accuracy and the helpfulness of my reading. Even my high school English teacher, Mr. Powers, heard that I did palm readings and asked me to read his palm.

I gave him a short reading and he was hooked. During the school year he asked me to give him a reading on many occasions. (I like to believe, however, that the "A" I received in his course was due to my abilities as a student rather than as a palm reader.)

When I graduated from high school I enrolled as a journalism student at Boston University. I had never considered a career in journalism. However, my high school counselor had me fill out the Kuder Preference Inventory. He scored my results and told me the results indicated that journalism was, by far, the career that was best suited to my profile.

A few weeks into my freshman year, I received a note from Dr. Willem Pinard, the Chair of the Psychology Department. He requested that I come to his office for a meeting. When I arrived at the department, Pinard's secretary ushered me into the doctor's office and closed the door. Dr. Pinard, a tall and imposing figure, stood over me and scowled that he had heard I was giving palm readings for money. He told me that palmistry is a pseudoscience and that I was taking people's money under false pretenses. He commanded me to stop. During his scolding, I sat calmly and quietly. Finally, his tirade came to an end. Then I asked if I could look at his hands. He dutifully held out both hands and I proceeded to give him a short reading. When I finished, he didn't say anything. He just sat there, expressionless. I excused myself and left.

A few weeks later I received another note from Dr. Pinard who asked me to visit him again. This time he greeted me at the door and ushered me into his office. He closed the door, sat in a chair opposite me and held out his hands.

"Tell me more," he said.

I continued to read people's palms for money.

The highpoint of my adventure into professional palm reading occurred in my sophomore year. At that time, Dr. Stanley Jaks was the most famous mentalist in America. His agent also represented Eleanor Roosevelt, the wife of former President Franklin D. Roosevelt. Stanley and I had both published mentalism effects in the same issue of *The Linking Ring,* which is the official magazine of the International Brotherhood of Magicians. The organization had just awarded me a gold medal for my effect "Psychoanalysis."

One day I received a phone call from Stanley. He congratulated me on my effect and requested permission to perform it in his own shows.

I was thrilled at this opportunity to talk with the person I most admired in the field of mentalism, and I gave him permission to use my effect. It would be my honor. Stanley thanked me and said he often performed in Boston. He invited me to join him for dinner the next time he would be in town. A few weeks later I met him and we became very good friends until his untimely death several years later.

Stanley took a special interest in my palm reading. One of his subsequent trips to Boston coincided with my appearance at a charity fair. At the event, I read each client's palm in a booth enclosed by curtains. Stanley sat outside where he couldn't see my client or me but he could hear our conversation through the curtains. Between clients, he and I discussed the reading that had just taken place. After I had completed five readings, Stanley made a strange suggestion.

"What do you think would happen if you deliberately read all the lines incorrectly on the next client's hand?" he asked.

He proposed that if the client's heart line indicated that she does not like to reveal her emotions, I should instead tell her she displays her emotions freely. If her head line showed that she was intuitive, I should tell her she is logical and rational. If her fate line says that she will have one career throughout her life, I should tell her she has had many different jobs and will continue to keep changing her career path.

My first reaction was to reject this suggestion. I felt a special obligation to my clients and it would be unethical for me to deliberately provide wrong information to a trusting client. On the other hand, I respected Stanley. He was a trusted and wise friend.

Reluctantly, I decided to give his suggestion a try.

My next client was a lady who told me she had received readings from many other palmists. After the usual chit chat, I began the reading. Her head line indicated she was intuitive. However, I told her she was rational and logical. Her heart line indicated she expressed her emotions openly, but I told her she hides her emotions from others. Her sun line indicated she was artistic and inventive. Instead, I told her she was practical and conventional.

As I gave her a reading that was purposefully wrong, I was startled and dismayed that she sat bolt upright, maintaining a rigid and unresponsive posture. This really spooked me. My clients usually provided feedback during a reading. I was sure that this faux reading had turned my client off, and I was ready to scold Stanley for convincing me to go through with this test.

When our session was over I asked my client what she thought of the reading. To my surprise, it turned out that she was *not* disappointed at all. Instead, she told me, she had been in shock. She was astonished by my accuracy. Everything I had said was spot on and she insisted that this was, by far, the very best reading she had ever experienced!

I continued to give false readings to my next few clients. I received similar responses. Despite the fact that I was deliberately providing them with incorrect interpretations of the signs in their hands, my clients uniformly reported the amazing accuracy of their readings.

This simple experiment demonstrated that all my previous readings provided no validity for palmistry. I quickly realized that whatever accounted for the success of my readings, it had nothing to do with the signs in my client's hands. The overwhelming success of my previous readings must be due to psychological processes that enabled the clients to make sense of the reading in terms of their personal concerns and background. Somehow, my clients were able to transform their readings into "accurate" accounts that provided meaning and inspiration for them.

The outcome of this test inspired me to change my major from journalism to psychology. I was hoping to find an explanation for why my clients accepted a reading as valid, regardless of whether it was based on a true or false reading using palmistry. Eventually I realized that my striking accuracy about "concrete" incidents was much less specific than it seemed at first. My readings allowed for a variety of possible interpretations by the client. The break in the heart line could indicate either a literal physical problem with the client's heart or a metaphorical "break up" of a relationship of some kind. If the client didn't recognize any such event, I could check the other lines to see if something else was indicated at that time. For example, I might find a marking on the headline that also corresponded with that same date. I could say that the difficulty might instead deal with a problem with the head or even some sort of confusion. In this manner, the number of possible ways to be correct about a "concrete" incident in the client's life was multiplied enormously.

I also learned that I would always succeed with a reading, and be able to transform even misses into hits, because believers want the reader to succeed. A believing client does not want to be responsible for a failed reading and so they make it fit.

During my six years working as a professional palm reader I originally transitioned from being a skeptic about the validity of palmistry to a believer. That is, until I discovered the accuracy of my readings was only an illusion. My readings invariably "succeeded" and I took each successful reading as further evidence for the validity of palmistry. If I had not been persuaded to deliberately provide false readings to my clients, I might never have discovered that all my "successful" readings didn't say anything about the validity of palmistry.

Psychic readers simply use their client's validation as evidence that their system works.

So I stopped reading palms for money. Then I devoted much of my life and career to investigating, exposing, and trying to defend the public from charlatans, fraudulent psychics, and scams of all sorts.

However, I still continue to read palms. In fact, I have been giving cold readings now for over seventy years. Most of these readings are performed for television shows or at conferences. I do this as a way to teach the general public about how psychic readings can powerfully affect our judgment and convince the most intelligent and wisest among us that something paranormal has happened. I see what takes place during a palm reading as an example of how smart people can be seduced by the appeal of psychic readings.

Dr. Ray Hyman is a Professor Emeritus at the University of Oregon. Much of his work as an experimental and cognitive psychologist has been devoted to the psychology of deception and he is the only psychologist to have written a chapter on the psychology of deception for the *Annual Review of Psychology*. Ray is the author of numerous articles and several books including *The Nature of Psychological Inquiry* and *The Elusive Quarry: A Scientific Appraisal of Psychical Research*. He is the founder of the *Skeptic's Toolbox*, an annual four-day workshop devoted to teaching critical thinking.

On (And Off) The Rocks

Lynne Kelly

There was no spiral carved into the rock. I looked and looked and it was definitely not there. Half an hour later, I returned to look again and the spiral was perfectly clear. I had quietly laughed at the warning that this would happen.

Now I'm simply baffled.

My Ph.D. research involved looking at the way indigenous cultures have used a wide variety of devices to memorize all the information on which their survival depended. Without a system of writing, they were dependent on the same unreliable memory that regularly fails you and me. The only difference is that they were dependent on their fragile memories to record all the knowledge learned over generations while we can just write it down. Not surprisingly, indigenous cultures developed, over hundreds and thousands of years, a vast array of highly effective memory technologies. It is those mnemonic systems that fascinate and astound me.

I've always railed against the common representation of indigenous cultures living in a fog of superstition. I was convinced that in order to survive they needed to know a great deal about plants, animals, seasonal variations, navigational routes, genealogy, laws, resource rights, land management, and the list goes on. As my Australian Aboriginal Warlpiri colleague, Nungarrayi, counseled me, using a familiar term of endearment: "The Elders were pragmatic old buggers. We wouldn't have survived if they weren't."

But without writing, how on earth did they memorize so much stuff?

Well, here's one example. Scientists have documented the Navajo classification of over 700 insects along with descriptions of the critters, their habitat and behavior. Of these 700, only one was eaten and a few more were known because they were pests to either livestock or edible plants. The rest were known because the Navajo are human and humans love to organize knowledge. An entire invertebrate field guide was stored in memory. And that's just insects.

I soon discovered that indigenous cultures the world over memorized vast amounts of information using abstract symbols as memory aids with which they could encode layer upon layer of practical knowledge. Granted, they also encoded spiritual beliefs but it was the rational information that was my research focus. In all the contemporary and historical oral cultures I studied, their knowledge was encoded in mythology; it was sung and danced and performed in ceremonies because vivid stories, songs, and dances are so much easier to remember than bare facts in prose. In my field of primary orality, mythology is considered primarily as a mnemonic device, while not denying its complexity.

What many people misconstrue as nebulous indigenous ceremonies in fact represent the repetition of the songs, dances, and mythology to ensure that practical information is not lost. Alongside these performances there is a universal use of the method of loci, the way in which information is associated with specific locations. In classical times, from Homer to Cicero and then right through the Renaissance, the most powerful memory method known to humans was taught in schools and practiced extensively. The information to be memorized would be associated with a sequence of locations around a building or down a street—a door, then a pillar, then a window... To recall the information, the orator or student would simply imagine themselves walking from location to location and withdrawing the information associated with each position in sequence. The reason this works extraordinarily well is linked to the way the human brain functions and is why all modern memory champions still use this technique. None better has been found. So it was no wild leap when my research suggested that all oral cultures, totally dependent on their memories for everything they knew, were using exactly the same method. It wasn't a Greek invention at all.

I argued that Australian Aboriginal songlines, Native American pilgrimage trails, Inca ceques and other structures set out through the landscape were totally pragmatic versions of the method of loci. I also experimented with my own memory locations set within the house, the garden, and around the block. I was astounded by how effectively the method worked. Suddenly I could remember masses of information as long as it was structured and I had imagined vivid stories to link the information to the location. I was creating my own mythology. It was, without doubt, a pale reflection of indigenous mythology, but as a memory aid, it was superb.

Indigenous cultures incorporated abstract symbols as mnemonic aids—they painted these on bark, carved them into trees, and printed them on cloth. We know this, because they told us so. Australia Aboriginal cultures and Native American peoples used spirals in a multitude of contexts as part of their hugely practical memory systems. Part of my research involved applying my understanding of indigenous mnemonics to the archaeological record. In Peru, the Nasca laid out huge spirals in the desert. Despite von Däniken's claim that the huge animals and geometric shapes on the desert could only be seen from the air (created, of course, for aliens to see), they could also be seen from nearby hills. Archaeologists have shown that they were designed to be walked and not necessarily viewed at all. There were spirals on the megaliths of Malta, on the huge carved stones at Neolithic Newgrange in Ireland, on the Orkney Islands, north of Scotland, and in the ancient rock art of Chaco Canyon in New Mexico, which is my favorite archaeological site in the world.

I was really into spirals.

This was why, in 2009, I went to New Mexico to study contemporary Pueblo cultures and Ancestral Puebloan archaeology. At the Petroglyph National Monument on the outskirts of Albuquerque, about 24,000 images were carved into the soft volcanic rock by the Ancestral Pueblo people and early Spanish settlers. I was keen to see if the Pueblo petroglyphs matched the pattern I would expect if they were being used as part of a set of memory locations. Each of the incised rocks should be separated from its neighbor with the sequence clearly defined. My long-awaited excursion to the site proved to be more complicated than I had planned.

I don't enjoy driving in Australia, but at least we drive on the left side of the road. There was no way I was going to drive in America on the 'wrong' side, so I decided to walk from my hotel to the Monument. Due to incompetence (I'm struggling to come up with any better explanation) I read the distance in kilometers, as it is in Australia, instead of the miles marked on American maps. Consequently, my walk took me an hour longer than expected and I arrived just as the park was closing. I begged for a few minutes to dash outside and photograph a few images. The nearest petroglyphs were a short drive away, the interpretive officer, Diane, patiently explained. Not a walk, but a drive. The Americans I met during my entire trip were endlessly accommodating but Diane surpassed any reasonable expectation. She said she still had some work to do and, after a brief chat about my purpose in being there, suggested a particular path among the petroglyphs. She would drive me there and leave me alone among the rocks, collecting me an hour later.

Diane gave me two warnings. Firstly, watch out for rattlesnakes. And secondly, the Native Americans had explained that some of the petroglyphs will only appear if they want you to see them. She assured me that she was totally rational but had experienced this herself. I nodded respectfully managing, I sincerely hope, to conceal my smirk. I started walking up the path photographing the petroglyphs. Exactly as expected, they were beautifully spaced along the path so that each would be encountered separately. They had the combination of abstract and representational forms that my theory predicted.

I was pathetically excited when I saw a sign for a spiral.

The sign stood proudly next to a beautiful rock on which there was absolutely, definitely, undoubtedly *no* spiral. I looked on every side and at every nearby rock although it was absolutely clear on which surface I should be seeing the shape. I checked a few times from different angles in case it was a trick of the light, but nothing I did revealed a spiral on that rock. I dutifully photographed the empty space. Then I walked on for another quarter of an hour or so along the path seeing each carving exactly as described by its little sign. I turned and walked back down the track and stood in front the spiral-less rock.

There was a spiral.

Spiral Petroglyph
(Photo: Lynne Kelly)

The spiral was absolutely clear, exactly as represented on its sign. I took more photographs. I tried different angles to see if I could make the spiral disappear through tricks of the light, but it was always there, mocking me. The spiral was visible in both sets of photos. I returned to Diane's office and confessed my experience. She just smiled knowingly. At no stage did she offer me a spiritual or psychic explanation. She was as confused by this occurrence as I was, just far more accepting. Meanwhile, she had searched out an enormous document for me on Native American interpretations of the petroglyphs. She saved me the long walk back by driving me to my hotel, taking the scenic route to show me the glorious Rio Grande.

I have found throughout my research that I have an unexpectedly strong emotional reaction to the inanimate objects I have used in memory experiments mimicking the indigenous devices. I have a particularly strong attachment to an Australian Aboriginal object, a coolamon, which came to me via Nungarrayi. This food-carrying wooden dish is engraved on the back with abstract signs, which Nungarrayi explained were used as a mnemonic aid for multiple layers of "women's business." This practical knowledge would have been taught to the girl who carried it well over 100 years ago. In Nungarrayi's terms, the coolamon chose *me* as a conduit from the Ancestors to get the message out about Aboriginal intellect. I can rationally justify my attachment to this object because of the circumstances and ceremony in which it was conveyed to my keeping. I must admit, however, that this is a completely different feeling to that I have about the object's sentimental value. But I can rationalize my response if I try really hard.

However, I cannot explain my mysterious experience with the Ancestral Puebloan spiral.

Dr. Lynne Kelly is an Australian writer, researcher, and science communicator and she is an Honorary Research Associate at LaTrobe University, Melbourne. Lynne is the author of sixteen books, including *The Skeptic's Guide to the Paranormal* and *The Memory Code: The Traditional Aboriginal Memory Technique That Unlocks the Secrets of Stonehenge, Easter Island and Ancient Monuments the World Over.* www.lynnekelly.com.au

The Ghostly Soldier And The Phantom Footsteps

Greg Laden

As we moved into the guest quarters of the McGregor Museum, we received a warning.

"You're a scientist, like I am," said the archaeologist who lived downstairs. As he spoke, my students carted luggage and equipment up to the apartment, complaining about the effort. "So I understand if you don't believe me, but…"

"… But what?" I asked, as I glanced up the stairs, concerned the students were taking the good rooms for themselves.

"The place is haunted."

I stared in disbelief.

"The Norwegian scientists visiting last month were supposed to stay for three weeks," he continued, "but they left after only five days."

Seriously?

"The ghost drove them out," he said. "Oh, by the way, avoid the bedroom that is an extension of the hallway."

"Why?"

"Just *avoid* it."

So I went upstairs and the students had indeed taken the two best bedrooms, set our lab equipment up in the third bedroom, and dumped my luggage in the dreaded bedroom that I was supposed to avoid.

That night, everyone was pretty tired, which was good, because when the disembodied footsteps came walking down the hallway—and back and forth a couple of times—I think I was the only person who heard them.

Many people died in Kimberly, South Africa, during the siege of October 14, 1899, that lasted through February 15, 1900. This building, the modern day McGregor Museum, was the military headquarters at the time. Later it became an infirmary, and it was said that many died in these very bedrooms, where we were staying. For a long time Kimberly was a frontier diamond-mining town, where arms dealers, slavers, smugglers, and mercenaries carried out their nefarious activities, so the homicide rate was pretty high. The 1918 influenza epidemic was bad here too. In other words, there was no shortage of raw material for ghost stories.

McGregor Museum
(Photo: The Heritage Portal)

Added to that, and of concern to my students, was the fact that we were spending most of the summer poking our noses into dangerous places, from a ghostly view. A large area of previously unmapped graves had been discovered a few blocks away, and was currently being investigated by the McGregor Museum archaeology staff. There were numerous skeletons found in systematically dug graves, some tossed haphazardly into perfectly dug rectangular pits, some lowered into coffins. For reasons unknown, most of the skulls had been sawn through to remove the brains. Some graves held one body, others housed several. It seems that the grave diggers produced one perfect pit every day and used that for whoever happened along.

That same archaeology crew had just been down in Cape Town dealing with more accidentally exposed graves. And the site we were excavating that summer appeared to have a bushmen grave cairn on it, which ultimately proved to have no bones of the dead, but a rather large living scorpion.

So, the ghost walking up and down the hall pretty much fit in with the summer's theme, and the town's theme, of abundant death and misery.

The morning after I first heard the ghostly footsteps, my colleague Lynne, who had slept in the lab room, raised the familiar topic.

"Greg, your students are really afraid of ghosts," she said.

"Why were they even talking about ghosts?" I asked.

"They've talked about little else since finding out that ghost tours are the biggest business in town! And sooner or later they're going to hear whatever was walking up and down the hall last night."

So she had heard the mysterious footsteps too.

"Nah," I replied. "They'll just get drunk and pass out every night as usual. Don't worry about it."

"We'll see. What do you suppose was pacing the hall anyway? I looked out of my room but saw nothing," she said a little too casually.

"Everything has a scientific explanation, my dear friend," I said.

"Somehow I knew you were going to say that."

Lynne was right. Both students harbored strong beliefs in ghosts. And, we quickly realized that our temporary abode was indeed on the route of the local ghost tours. These tours are one of the biggest businesses in Kimberly. The buses traveled around the city taking people to various haunted houses. One evening, we saw a van pitch up just outside the Museum. Several tourists climbed out, and the guide pointed in our direction, presumably telling stories about the ghostly inhabitants. My students hastily covered themselves in bed sheets and danced back and fourth in an apparitional fashion, passing between the numerous windows, with the hallway lights flashing on and off. Pretty soon the tourists piled back into the van and drove off at a fast clip.

And, eventually, the students heard the "thing" walking down the hallway.

We had all heard the sound of phantom footsteps, moving along the creaky floors, retracing their steps, trudging along steadily and slowly. But if you looked down the hall there would be nothing there. The footsteps also seemed to stop if you opened a door or made any noise. Even so, the students refused to use the bathroom at night. This is how it was for a couple of weeks.

As mentioned, I occupied the "hallway extension" room. To get into the apartment, I would walk up a set of stairs and through a lockable doorway. Then to the right was a bedroom, and to the left a bathroom. Moving on ahead down the hallway were two more bedrooms on the right for a total of three. On the left side past the bathroom was a kitchen. Then, at the end of the hall, it took a left and went up a step, and continued on for fifteen feet until it met a door that was always locked. We were told that we should never attempt to open it.

That L-shaped part of the hallway—the extension—was wide enough to fit a narrow bed, and a second door had been fitted at the beginning of it.

That was my room.

The first night, I was sitting in my bedroom when the light suddenly went out. I assumed the bulb had blown. I looked around for a new bulb but did not find one.

I forgot about the incident. The next day while I was preparing to go out to the field site, the light mysteriously turned on. Then I heard footsteps on the other side of the door that was not to be opened. I went over to the door and peered in through the keyhole. I could barely make out what looked like the form of a 19th century chap in a uniform of the style that would have been worn by a Royal Scots Dragoon Guard, kilt and all, at the time of the Siege.

Was I looking at a ghost?

What the hell was going on?

But I soon developed a theory. Later that night, after a day in the field, I went to my room intentionally at a certain time, turned on the light and waited. Soon enough, I heard footsteps on the other side of the door that was not to be opened, and in a moment, the light went off. And away walked the footsteps.

The next day, after getting back from the field a bit earlier, I went round to the entrance of the Museum's public galleries, talked my way past the ticket taker, and hopped up the stairs along one of the old Infirmary's wings. At the top of the stairs was a large room, where several patrons were admiring the glass cases with mannequins of men in the various uniforms that dated to the time of the siege of Kimberly. One was in a kilt. Near the back of the room was a Gatling gun on display, and behind this, there was a locked door. Next to the door was a light switch.

**The "Ghostly" Soldier
(Photo: Greg Laden)**

I walked over to the light switch and turned it off. The lights in the Museum room went off. I got on my hands and knees and peered through the old keyhole of the door, but I couldn't see anything. So I reached up to the light switch and flipped it on, and suddenly I could see my room through the keyhole, and all of my personal effects spread out across the bed. "Hmm," I remember thinking, "I should keep my room neat because I'm on public display here."

As I stood to leave, I turned to the people who had been looking at the mannequins and said, "You know, this place is haunted!"

"I know!" they said in unison, their eyes wide.

So, that explained the mysterious "haunted" light and the "ghost" of the kilted soldier I saw through the keyhole.

But it didn't explain the phantom footsteps.

One morning I got up early, an hour before sun-up, to shave before going out on the field. The lighting in the bathroom was poor, but there was a security spotlight outside the window. So I opened the frosted glass pane to let in a little more light.

As I was starting to scrape the razor against my face, I heard the ghostly footsteps walking down the hall—away from me. Then I heard the preternatural footfalls coming back the other way. Slowly, deliberately, the steps grew closer and closer until they paused right by the bathroom door.

I was just about to swing open the door to see what the heck was out there, when suddenly a sound came from outside the bathroom window. I turned, rather startled, just in time to see a giant furry cat drop from the roof onto a nearby ledge. Leaping, she came in through the bathroom window and landed directly on the bathroom sink. Without an introduction of any kind, she insisted that I pet her. So I did. After a minute of petting, she became bored and leaped out of the window onto the ledge, then back onto the roof of the building. From there, she walked to the other end of the roof over the guest quarter's hallway.

Now I could explain the ghostly footsteps that had haunted us all these days and, indeed, driven the Norwegians to alternative accommodation.

There were joints in the metal roof. As the cat pitter-pattered along the roof in her feline fashion, she would come to these joints along the roof and they would creak or ping. This was just like walking along a creaking floor, which will occasionally let out a sound depending on where you step, but much more regularly. It sounded like footfalls: Like ghostly, preternatural, disembodied footfalls.

So, the ghost was a cat walking back and forth on the roof, looking for an opening into the building. And finally, I gave her one. And she came in through the bathroom window.

For the rest of the day, I couldn't get that song out of my head.

Dr. Greg Laden is an archaeologist and biological anthropologist who earned his Ph.D. from Harvard University. He has taught at many institutions including Harvard, the University of Minnesota and Boston University. He is currently a freelance writer and science communicator at ScienceBlogs where he writes about paleoanthropology, global warming and evolution. http://scienceblogs.com/gregladen/

I'm Not Saying It Was Aliens But...

Dean Learner

I remember the incident like it happened yesterday. I felt the leather couch beneath me but at the same time I was somewhere else. The hypnotherapist who led me through the memory regression was well known. I remember choosing her because all of those TV documentaries about alien abduction said she was the best.

This session with her was all I needed to recall those crazy events that took place several years ago and the story unfolded as it flowed effortlessly out of my mouth. Before, all I had were questions. Now, I had answers.

One afternoon when I was 17 I was lying on my bed reading *The Incredible Hulk* vol. 2, no. 140. Completely engrossed in the comic book, I barely heard my mother yell, "Dinner's ready!"

As I sat up I felt my head pass through some sort of membrane. I looked up and found myself inside what appeared to be an alien ship. Suddenly, I felt two sets of spindly hands grab my arms and shoulders and hoist me up onto a cold, table-like surface.

Three aliens stared down at me. They were the same type you'd find in abductee reports and Hollywood films: Large heads with big, almond-shaped eyes atop skinny, nude bodies.

I couldn't move. I just lay there on my back and watched as one of the aliens started to perform some sort of surgery on me while the others watched. This surgery seemed to be of the psychic variety. The "surgeon" didn't have a scalpel for cutting into my flesh; instead "he" sliced open my chest with simple hand waves. He held up a small, glowing egg-sized object and then attached it to one of my ribs. The aliens' hollow eyes seemed almost dead as they held their concentration on my chest. With another wave, my chest cavity closed back up and no stitch marks or scars were left behind. In retrospect, I should have felt terrified but I was strangely calm throughout the process.

(Image: Daniel Tarr)

Having completed their "surgery," they grabbed me by my arms and lifted me off the table. And in the next moment I was back in my bedroom. I heard my mother call out that I was about to miss dinner if I didn't get my butt into gear.

As I walked down the hallway to the dining room, I thought to myself about the amazing story I had to tell my best friend, Mike. However, by the time I reached the dinner table, I was left only with the thought that I was going to tell Mike about something incredible— but I couldn't remember what it was. Oh well, mom had made spaghetti! Not much else mattered at that point.

That night, I had a nagging feeling that I was forgetting something important. This worried me to the point of frustration. It felt like something was blocking my memory. I tried to remember what it was, but I only experienced a brief flashback every now and then.

The next day I was hanging out with Mike. He had managed to get his old, beat-up 1968 Yamaha motorcycle running again and we had no choice but to take it for a ride. We lived in a small rural town with lots of secluded roads to speed down. I was riding on the back of the motorcycle and I'm sure our combined weight was causing that poor 125cc engine to strain.

There was a large curve to the left in the road ahead. On the right side there was a soft dirt embankment and several large cottonwood trees. As we approached the curve I felt a presence behind me. I turned my head and was startled to see a large grey face with hollow black eyes staring back at me.

It was one of the aliens.

Suddenly, the rear wheel of the motorcycle was knocked out from under us. The bike went down. We went down. I hit the ground with my knees. I bounced and sailed above the road parallel to the pavement. Time seemed to slow down for me. I could see that Mike was traveling next to me. I watched as his body traveled head first towards a cottonwood tree. I foresaw the blood splatter as his skull cracked against the trunk. As he sailed through the air, I scooped my arm under his body and pulled him away from the tree. We both crashed into the embankment.

Groaning in pain, we stood up slowly and brushed the dirt off our clothes. With aching, bleeding knees we pushed the bike several miles back to my house. There, we used tweezers to pluck bits of gravel out of our knees, and then cleaned and bandaged ourselves up.

The next few days were uncomfortable. My legs were covered with scabs and I couldn't bend my knees. I walked like Frankenstein's monster. I tried to spend as much time as possible on the couch, enjoying the healing properties of potato chips while watching re-runs of "Gilligan's Island." My therapy was interrupted by a rustling sound outside. Shuffling to the window, I saw a golden retriever foraging through our garbage. I opened the front door and yelled at the animal but it didn't seem to hear. Waving my hands and shouting, I took my first stilted steps outside. The dog jumped away from me. I lunged towards it and it moved back exactly the same distance I had covered. We played this game for a while. It was futile. I just couldn't do a good chase without the use of my knees.

I found myself in the yard next door, where there was an empty house up for sale. As I passed by one of the windows I caught a glimpse of someone inside. I froze. No one should have been in that house, but as I placed my hands on the window and peered inside I saw someone tall, skinny, and grey. Next thing I knew, I was pushed hard. I fell forward into the glass window and it shattered.

(Image: Locklip)

The thick shards of glass sliced my wrist and thumb severely. I watched in shock as the blood started spurting forth rhythmically like I had only seen in horror movies. Once I made it back to my house, I wrapped my wrist tightly in a handkerchief. I applied as much pressure as I could before collapsing on the couch with the phone in my hand. I felt myself growing drowsy as I dialed the first phone number that came to mind. In my state, 911 didn't occur to me.

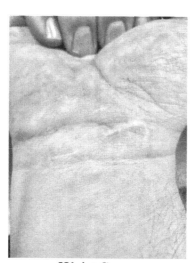

Wrist Scars
(Photo: Dean Learner)

My ex-girlfriend answered.

"Hello?"

"Hey..."

"How are you?" she asked. "I haven't spoken to you in a while!"

"I'm just hanging out here...bleeding to death..."

"WHAT?"

Within minutes she was there to rush me to the emergency room where I was stitched back together.

I never saw the aliens again.

How could I explain this strange experience?

Well, according to the hypnotherapist, I had somehow pierced the veil into another dimension and stumbled upon an alien spaceship that was engaged in dimensional travel. The aliens attached a tracking device to my chest to make sure I didn't report this incident to other humans and then they administered some kind of memory suppression. As it wore off and I started remembering the incident, they gave a show of force to shut me up.

I have had my chest x-rayed and scanned but the lump doesn't show up. However, you can feel it. It is clearly there. Beyond getting a biopsy, the doctors shrug their shoulders. It's not bone, cartilage, or a calcium deposit.

Of course, this doesn't mean that it is alien either.

After my session with the hypnotherapist, I was baffled by the bizarre story I'd told and the vivid memories that accompanied it. She provided me with a recording of the session and when I listened to it I was left with a different feeling: Anger. She had asked numerous leading questions to manipulate me into inventing a fantasy about alien abduction.

"How did you get onto the alien ship?" she asked.

"What did the aliens do to you when they put you on that table?"

"Where did the aliens put the implant?"

"When did the aliens attack you again?"

In her life's work, psychologist Elizabeth Loftus has shown that repressed memory therapy, hypnosis, past-life regression, guided visualization and other related practices are dangerous for their tendencies to create false narratives. These therapies have lead to the creation of false memories and confabulations of sexual molestation, satanic ritual abuse, and alien abductions.

Leading questions and suggestions from the therapist are prone to influence a client who is vulnerable, such as those worried that they may have been abducted by aliens. People in this suggestible state will often put together the pieces of the puzzle until the details of the "alien abduction" become clear to them. Memories that are created under hypnosis are indistinguishable from real memories and can even be more vivid.

I was just another notch on the hypnotherapy couch of this woman to prove her theory: That humans are being visited, abducted, and tested on by space aliens.

I felt violated.

The only thing I can't explain is the real chain of events that left me with scars on my knees and wrist, and a lump on my chest, which is fastened firmly to my rib bone.

So I still have questions.

Dean Learner (a pseudonym) has debated alleged alien abductees and their hypnotherapists on CNN, The Travel Channel, NBC, CBS, the ABC and elsewhere.

The Lucky Coin

Matt Lowry

Some of us deliberately avoid stepping on cracks in the pavement or walking under ladders. Perhaps we wear our underpants inside out for good luck, or make a wish before blowing out the candles on our birthday cake. Maybe we refuse to say "Macbeth" in a theater, or we knock on wood to stave off bad luck.

We're all human and, despite any skeptical leanings, we all have some aspects to our lives about which we're decidedly non-skeptical. On the TV show "Bullshit!" magician Penn Jillette once summed it up by saying: "Everybody got a gris-gris" (pronounced gree-gree). He meant that we all have some kind of belief, superstition or viewpoint we hold onto that is irrational. A gris-gris is a blind spot in our thinking.

In a literal sense, gris-gris refers to a Voodoo charm. It is a magical bag or doll that is a portable spell. A grig-gris can contain herbs, powders, shells, bones, and graveyard dust, or a prayer written on a piece of paper. A grig-gris may take the form of a talisman that attracts good luck, or an amulet that wards off evil, among other things. But we don't have to believe in Voodoo to have a lucky charm. Dangerous and stressful situations can increase our superstitiousness. During World Wars I and II, American soldiers carried "Letters from Heaven," a kind of chain-letter that was believed to protect them from harm. Some people still carry a rabbit's foot or wear an item of jewelry for good luck. Students wear lucky socks to exams and many athletes have lucky objects and rituals they believe will help them to win the game.

Sometimes a gris-gris takes the form of a ritual or habit, loyalty to a particular brand of item (from cars to skin cream), the support of a sports team, a religious belief, or affiliation with a political party. Whatever it may be, our gris-gris is very important to us, yet we may not even think of it as strange, and we can behave in decidedly unreasonable ways when confronted with the possibility that our gris-gris is just another silly belief unsupported by evidence.

There is a popular anecdote about physicist and Nobel laureate Niels Bohr. A friend visited Bohr and was surprised to find a horseshoe hanging above the front doorway of the scientist's home—tradition saying that a horseshoe attracts good luck when placed with the ends pointed up above a door. He couldn't help but comment.

"Niels," he said, "It can't be possible that you, a brilliant scientist, believe in that foolish horseshoe superstition!"

"Of course I don't believe in it," Bohr replied. "But I understand it brings you good luck, whether you believe in it or not."

The story is apocryphal—it is also attributed to Albert Einstein and Carl Alfred Meier—but the point is that if we look hard enough, I'm pretty sure that every one of us can find at least one gris-gris that we cling to—if we'll admit it to ourselves.

To illustrate this point I would like to share with you my gris-gris: I have a "lucky" coin.

It is an Eisenhower Dollar that I inherited from Herschel, my wife's paternal grandfather. I can't say that the coin has ever brought me good luck or prevented me from bad luck, but it has great sentimental value. This is because I received it after he had died, and the fact that my wife's family had accepted me so completely into their fold. It is also meaningful to me because I've always had a love for space exploration, and this coin features an eagle landing on the moon with Earth in the background. This is a reference to Neil Armstrong's famous words uttered when the Eagle, the craft carrying him and his fellow crew members, landed on the moon: "The Eagle has landed." In addition, this coin was minted in 1972—the year of my birth.

The Lucky Coin
(Photo: Matt Lowry)

I carry the coin with me everywhere I go. In fact, I often catch myself feeling inside my pocket to make sure that it's still there. I take comfort in its presence and the knowledge that it hasn't magically disappeared. I will go so far as to say that if I can't find the coin to put into my pocket at the beginning of the day, I drop everything to start looking for it. A couple of times I have been late for work because I was tearing my house apart to find my lucky coin. And if I'm forced to leave home without it, I get cold sweats.

I know it's just a silly superstition and there's no rational reason to think the coin is lucky—but I still believe it. Why? Because it's a habit, and on some level it gives me comfort and strength.

I've made this confession publicly at skeptical events, as a way to further the discussion about how we all have a gris-gris. In September 2011, I attended the Dragon*Con convention in Atlanta, Georgia. I spoke on a panel where I shared my belief in my lucky coin. This led to a skeptical intervention of sorts during the Q&A session, when non-theist activist Margaret Downey stood up and asked if I would be willing to give up my lucky coin for one day (she offered to keep it safe for me). With much groaning and gnashing of teeth, I reluctantly handed over my gris-gris to Margaret for that entire day.

At first I was really, really nervous about not having my coin with me, but eventually I started to feel less anxious (though I never stopped thinking about it). The next day, when Margaret and I met, my precious gris-gris was returned to me, and things somehow seemed better.

A few years later, I actually *lost* my lucky coin. The first few days were very uncomfortable for me, but reflecting on how Margaret had weaned me off my gris-gris for that one day helped. Eventually I learned how to get along without it, thinking about it only occasionally. Nine months after I lost the coin, I found it hiding in an obscure corner of my closet, and as I type this story it sits safely in my hip pocket.

Just as I have my gris-gris I have come to understand that everyone has their own gris-gris that is precious and dear to them. It was very uncomfortable to have my coin taken from me by Margaret Downey and later, by pure happenstance, so I can relate to those who hold on to certain beliefs that are challenged by meddlesome skeptics. As Margaret challenged me to give up my coin, skeptics challenge peoples' beliefs and practices—be they ghosts, UFOs, religion, or whatever—to get them to give up something that is precious to them. In many cases, these beliefs form part of the identity of the believer, so that when someone challenges that belief, these people feel that their very identity is also being challenged. By acknowledging that we skeptics can have our own personal gris-gris too, we can learn to sympathize with other people and their beliefs.

We can look at a gris-gris as an irrational belief, superstition, or theory that we don't want to give up yet. Perhaps there's nothing wrong with having a gris-gris, if we acknowledge that it is just a gris-gris, and that, like my "lucky" coin, it's harmless and simply makes us feel better. Or maybe some of us aren't even aware that we have a gris-gris. Then it's a matter of recognizing it, and learning how to control our superstitious thinking, rather than being controlled by it.

I suspect there's a lesson in here somewhere. But I have to remind myself: After writing this story, I'm still carrying my lucky coin in my hip pocket. Oh well, baby steps…

So, what's your gris-gris?

Matt Lowry is a high school teacher and college physics professor with a strong interest in promoting science education, skepticism, and critical thinking among his students and the population in general. Towards these ends, he worked with the James Randi Educational Foundation on their educational advisory board, and he has also worked with a number of grassroots skeptical, pro-science groups. He blogs on these and related subjects at The Skeptical Teacher. https://skepticalteacher.wordpress.com

Beyond A Joke

Mike McRae

Twenty years ago, I was a vampire.

I only ever came out at night.

I snuck into people's rooms as they slept.

I sucked their blood ...

And then I ran it through a bunch of diagnostic machines to determine blood cell count, electrolyte levels, and liver enzymes.

It was a rare honor for a clinical laboratory scientist such as myself to interact personally with the patients. Charged with working the night shift at Pindara Private Hospital on the Gold Coast of Queensland, Australia, I was a one-man-show. Cost-cutting measures meant that I didn't have a phlebotomist to call on, so I had to take blood from the patients myself. I would pack a small bag with latex gloves and vacu-tubes and attend to accident and emergency patients convinced they had appendicitis, intensive care patients who were more plastic tubes than flesh, and help out in the occasional late night ward to curry favor with the overworked nurses.

Pindara Hospital
(Photo: Pindara Private Hospital)

Sticking syringes into people isn't a natural talent, though it slowly became a skill in which I took pride. Living at night also had its downsides. On the plus side, patients who were usually barcodes and signatures on the sides of test tubes became names and faces. I had the opportunity to hear their stories, listen to their fears, and read the results from the assays in shades of human emotion, of relief and disappointment.

A sad reality of nocturnal life in a hospital is that I'd occasionally come across a dead body, a patient who had recently passed in peaceful slumber. It was uncommon, but an experience you don't forget in a hurry. Meeting them *after* they'd died, though, wasn't something I was used to, vampire or not. So my mysterious conversation with Filthy Jack is an encounter worthy of telling.

Jack wasn't his real name, and, I confess, whatever he called himself is long forgotten, but we'll call him that to preserve his dignity. Given that I do remember his propensity for profanity and crude humor, "Filthy" will suit him just fine. It was never uncommon for the older folk to tell a blue joke or two as you busied yourself with sorting tubes and tourniquet. I even had a 90-something old woman want to tell me a joke on her intensive care deathbed while the cardiologist struggled to get her to lay still for an ECG. ("It's a bit smutty," she said, "But they're the best sort.") But old Jack was something else. "Did I tell you the one about the prostitute and the judge? Or the one about the virgin walking into the bar?" I had heard these jokes, and wished I hadn't, but Filthy would give me a rerun anyway, winking one jaundiced eye as if it was our little secret.

Waking up patients was never a fun part of the job. Nobody likes to be startled awake at two in the morning with a syringe diving under their skin, so I'd do my best to give my clients a little shake before going about any needle business. Filthy needed no such warning: Whether he was a night owl like me, or merely an insomniac, for the entire month he was always waiting up with reading material in one hand and a coffee in a Styrofoam cup in the other. Sometimes he'd be reclining in a chair in his room, soft-core porn magazine splayed over his lap. Sometimes he'd be shuffling down the corridors. Once or twice I ran into him outside, smelling faintly of an illicitly inhaled cigarette.

So it was hardly a surprise when I bumped into Filthy on my way to the emergency department early one night. I pre-empted his usual greeting by telling him that he'd better have a clean joke for me later on, only to receive a big grin as I continued on to exsanguinate an OD, or a heart attack, or a drunk pulled from a car wreck. Unfortunately, I no longer recall the exact sequence of the joke itself, but as I passed him by the old man gave it a good shot with one about two nuns and a bike. I told Jack I'd come back for the punch line, expecting to poke his vein during my 1:30 a.m. round as I had every other night that week.

Sadly, Filthy Jack never got the chance to deliver his punch line. When I arrived in his room at 1:45 a.m., his bed was empty. Fresh, crisp white sheets were folded tight, and the air smelled of antiseptic. The lights and television were switched off. Apparently, his body was already cold in the morgue. Jack had been refrigerated when I clocked on at 10:30 p.m. According to the nurse on duty, his body had been chilling in there seventeen hours prior that morning as well. Filthy had died shortly after my shift had ended the previous sunrise.

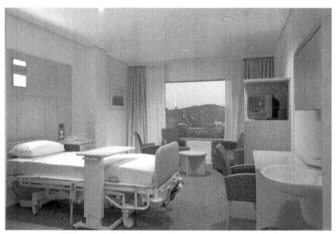

(Photo: Pindara Private Hospital)

"Are you sure?" I asked the matron on the desk at the front of his ward.

She checked a folder and nodded. "Yes. They took him out quarter past seven this morning."

"But I saw him out front just a few hours ago…"

People have a certain look when you say things like that. It's a slow blink with open eyes, while the melancholic organ tune from the "Twilight Zone" plays hauntingly in the background.

"I don't know what to tell you," she said, clearly knowing exactly what to tell me, if only her mother hadn't raised her to act with etiquette. "Cardiac arrest this morning. Sorry, we should have canceled his 1:30 a.m. bleed."

At that time of my life I wasn't yet what you'd call a "skeptic," even though the seeds of critical thinking were germinating. Nonetheless, my conviction of having spoken to Filthy Jack was strong and the cognitive dissonance brought on by the news of his demise was disorienting. The impact of that moment stuck with me for many years, leaking out after a few beers at the bar when competing with others over who had the scariest story. It didn't win me any titles—everybody gets distracted by the nuns coming on their bicycle—but it felt to me like a legitimate ghost story.

Was it the soul of Filthy Jack prowling those corridors, searching for victims to amuse with a dirty stand-up routine? Though nearly two decades have since passed, I can still remember the certainty of it being Jack sitting in that chair, looking washed out in the too-blue, too-white glow of the fluorescent light. Shaggy mop of white hair, striped pajamas, barely shaven, and yellowing face: I had no doubt it was Filthy Jack.

But the problem is, I have this medical condition.

Prosopagnosia is commonly referred to as face-blindness. According to one German study, up to 2.5 percent of the population could suffer from this disorder which involves the fusiform gyrus—a blueberry sized nub of nervous tissue in the parietal lobe of the brain. This structure is responsible for processing visual data and quickly producing a sense of familiarity in known faces, or alarm with unknown ones. Apparently, it does a similar trick with cars, and makes navigation a problem, but those are horror stories for another time.

Like many with a mild case of this inability, in my early twenties I didn't know I suffered from it. To me, others merely had super powers of lightning quick human identification. I was slow, sure, but doesn't everybody confuse actors Gerard Butler with Jeremy Renner? Place a person out of context, and I am either slow to recognize them or quick to mistaken them. As a teacher, I made careful use of seating plans and school diaries to keep track of the students in uniform, forgoing duties that required me to name students out of context. My wife and son, coincidentally passing by me in a local supermarket one afternoon, were strangers blurred into the crowd until I remembered the clothes they wore that morning. Without a name to put to my unusual quirk of poor pattern matching, I unconsciously adapted by using other clues to identify people, such as clothing, hairstyles, and speech patterns.

Today, I'm embarrassingly aware of my struggle to link a face with a name. I have no doubt my life, pre-diagnosis, was full of errors in association, which people politely ignored as I naively continued to call them by the wrong name.

It's almost certain that the ghostly figure of Filthy Jack was a random patient in striped pajamas who took interest in my friendly smile, and responded happily to my suggestion of a joke with one about nuns on bikes. After all, the man's mop of hair and failed liver complexion was hardly out of place in an institution full of dirty old ex-alcoholics, and facial features such as the hollow curves of his cheeks, the drooping of his eyes, an aquiline nose, a mole, liver spots, and cob webs of wrinkles, wouldn't trigger my mind to distinguish Jack from John.

Of course, even as a skeptic, I refuse to rule out the possibility that the ghost of the old prankster was eager to tell me just one more joke from beyond the grave. However, that's unlikely. I'm a science writer who understands physics and biology, and I know how our minds can make mistakes.

But sometimes I think about the incident and I regret cutting him off mid-joke. I like to think that Filthy's spirit lingered on for just a few more hours, severed from metabolism, yet clinging on to life as he waited forlornly, just to see my facial expression as he delivered the hilarious punch line, "It must be the cobblestones."

Mike McRae is no longer a clinical scientist sticking needles into people. Today he writes science articles for young adults, as well as the occasional science article for old children. Mike has written radio documentaries for Australia's ABC Radio National, and developed national and international education programs for the Australian government and other organizations. His book *Tribal Science: Brains, Beliefs, and Bad Ideas*, explores the development of modern science and the rise of pseudoscience. Mike splits his time between living in Sydney and San Francisco.

Strange Yet Familiar

Joe Nickell

Like everyone else, I've had some strange experiences. Some might say I've seen ghosts, encountered UFOs, and experienced the power of intuition. Here are several of my personal stories, together with some possible explanations for each.

My Grandmother's Ghost

My grandmother had a trunkful of costumes from school plays she helped stage, and she always encouraged my propensity for role-playing. From a young age I knew I would be a detective (I would later be trained in how to play roles as an undercover operative for a world-famous detective agency), so she gave me a big volume of the Sherlock Holmes stories and a Sherlockian deerstalker cap.

When I was in the seventh grade, she died. I adored my grandmother, and I grieved at her death. I remember thinking about her so much during this time that I felt I could sense her presence.

But I learned later in life that a memory could seem very real and be mistaken for an experience. This gave me personal insight into ghost sightings. I would eventually come to realize that seeing apparitions could occur not only as "waking dreams" (hallucinations that occur between wakefulness and sleep), but when one is tired, or daydreaming. An image might well up from the subconscious and be superimposed on the visual scene. Rather like a camera's double exposure, a "ghost" would be born.

In my career as a paranormal investigator, I have met many sincere people who have had mysterious experiences that led them to believe they had encountered ghosts. I have investigated many of these and have seen no evidence for an otherworldly realm.

Ghosts may not exist but the important thing is that we have our cherished memories of our lost loved ones.

The Haunted Chandelier

When investigating hauntings, I have been lucky to occasionally experience a ghostly effect myself.

I had one such spooky occurrence at the historic Hand Hotel in the mining town of Fairplay, Colorado. I had been asked to accompany a Denver high school teacher and her students on an overnight stay at this "haunted" location—as part of a class on critical thinking. We gathered in the lobby waiting to go out for dinner, when the chandelier's lights flickered mysteriously. A chorus of "Ooh!" and nervous laughter went up from the students.

The Hand Hotel
(Photo: TripAdvisor)

At that time, I just happened to have been watching the desk clerk when I saw him surreptitiously jiggle the light switch on the wall beside him. The teacher also witnessed this. Seeing us seeing him, the prankster returned a sheepish smile because he'd been caught red-handed.

The Vanishing Man

Many years ago, I witnessed something unusual. While driving in the countryside at night, I saw in my headlights a stooped old man by the roadside. Fearing he could be drunk and might step in front of my car, I slowed down and momentarily looked back to the highway. By the time I looked again the figure had vanished!

Upon closer inspection, it was only the silhouette of a tree stump with some branches and leaves that—from a particular angle—looked like the figure of a stooped old man. When I looked away, and then saw the object from a different view, the illusion was dispelled.

I have since learned much more about the mind's tendency to recognize familiar shapes in random patterns. Some people see images in tea leaves, pictures in clouds, ghosts or demons in the shadows in a photo, and "Bigfoot" in the woods. Such images are called simulacra, and the tendency to see them is known as pareidolia, a phenomenon by which the brain interprets vague images as specific ones. The "face" on Mars and the image of "Jesus" on a tortilla are famous examples.

The Face On Mars
(Photo: Wikipedia)

A Close Encounter

One day I saw a flying saucer—coming right at me!

I was startled for a moment, but I soon recognized it was only a commercial passenger plane that had taken off from an airport. When it first came into view above the tree line, it was heading directly toward me. I had seen the fuselage from the front rather than the side, with the wings positioned symmetrically on either side, to mimic the popular concept of a "flying saucer" seen in an edge view.

If someone who believed in UFOs and aliens had observed something like this from a distance—only to have it vanish by disappearing behind a cloud—it might well have been reported as a flying saucer.

The Santa Monica Lights

I have witnessed other UFOs—Unidentified Flying Objects—that became *identified* flying objects, after I had time to figure out what was happening.

The most bewildering of these was a strange array of lights I saw in the sky over Santa Monica, California, in the late 1970s. My first thought was that I had never seen anything like it nor would I ever see the phenomenon again. I certainly had witnessed a UFO, by definition.

To many enthusiasts, "UFO" is interchangeable with "alien craft." But we can't say: We don't know what the strange light is, so therefore it must be a vehicle from another planet. In other words, we can't draw a conclusion from "we don't know."

As it happened, the "Santa Monica Lights" proved to be of quite earthly origin—a terrestrial craft, in fact. The reasons it was so unidentifiable were twofold: the object was unfamiliar to me, and I was seeing it from an unfavorable view. When I kept looking and finally saw it from an intended view, I instantly recognized it as an advertising plane—not the daytime type towing a banner, but a nocturnal show of lights spelling out a message.

My Daughter's Intuition

In this final case, I didn't experience the sense of "intuition" but I was certainly a beneficiary.

In late 2003, I learned I was the biological father of a beautiful daughter, Cherie, who was then 36. Prior to finding this out, her "intuition" told her that she had a different father. When her mother asked her why she thought this she replied, "I don't know. It just came into my mind." A DNA test proved the relationship—a wonderful, life-transforming discovery—yet I was puzzled by her claim of intuition. With Cherie's help, I determined to investigate the mystery of how she came to "know" something she did not actually know.

**The Author and his Daughter
(Photo: Diana Harris)**

As it turned out, there were a number of clues that might have led to Cherie's sense of "knowing." She had a brother who was adopted, which raised the question of her own parentage. She held a resemblance to her mother, but not to the man she knew as her father, while her eyes resembled neither. These factors also suggested a different father. This possibility was reinforced when she learned, on her wedding day, that her parents were not married when she was conceived. Her mother, Diana, was my college sweetheart in 1966, but she suddenly left me to return to her previous boyfriend. She did not become pregnant, as she thought at the time, but already was so. And I believe there were more subtle clues as well, such as when Cherie asked her mother about her father and sensed an equivocation in her reply.

My friend, the late psychologist Robert A. Baker—responding specifically to this case—explained how we humans unconsciously collect bits of data that we assemble like puzzle pieces. When taken together, these clues can give us the sense of knowing something, without our having made a conscious effort. Such a revelation can seem quite mysterious. Of course, as experts on intuition warn, the process can yield faulty conclusions and even false memories. Nevertheless, I must admit to a new appreciation for the possibilities of intuition.

My life was changed forever by this discovery. I acquired a wonderful daughter, but also a family: Two grandsons, Chase and Tyner; later a granddaughter, Alexis Jo, who was named for me; and a wife—Diana and I married on April 1, 2006.

These stories show that mysterious experiences should invite neither uncritical belief in the supernatural, nor dismissal. Instead, we should always look for clues, and—with impartiality and a sincere desire for the truth—attempt to let the evidence lead us to the most likely solution. That is the one with the fewest unsubstantiated assumptions, according to the principle of Occam's razor. We should accept that simplest explanation, like it or not, until something comes along to warrant taking a new look.

Over a lifetime of following this approach I have come to believe that we live in a real and natural world.

Joe Nickell is one of the world's most famous skeptical paranormal investigators. He has investigated many high-profile cases, such as the diary of Jack the Ripper, the Nazca Lines in Peru, and the Shroud of Turin. He has written about numerous strange phenomena, including ghosts, Bigfoot, UFOs, religious miracles, and psychics, and he is the author or editor of over 30 books. These titles include *Secrets of the Supernatural: Investigating the World's Occult Mysteries; Missing Pieces: How to Investigate Ghosts, UFOs, Psychics, and Other Mysteries,* and *Tracking The Man-Beasts: Sasquatch, Vampires, Zombies, and More.* www.joenickell.com

A Stairway To Heaven

Massimo Polidoro

It was a pleasant mid-June afternoon sometime in the early 1980s. I was enjoying the tranquility of standing on the balcony of a country house in Pordenone in northern Italy. The sun was shining, birds were singing, and not a single cloud could be seen in the sky. Suddenly, I saw something unusual in the air. I thought it was a bird or a plane at first, but as I looked closely it didn't seem to be anything familiar. It was incredible.

It appeared to be a black three-stepped stairway in the middle of the sky. The lyrics of the song *"Stairway to Heaven"* by Led Zeppelin and the melodic *"Stairway to Paradise"* by Gershwin came to mind.

The mysterious object just hovered there in the air—I don't know how far from the ground—perfectly still. I was going to call somebody to confirm that what I was seeing was real and that I wasn't imagining it. Before I could do anything, the stairway became shorter and shorter until it suddenly vanished into thin air.

What the heck had I just seen? From what I knew about UFOs at the time, witnesses always described them as roundish objects, a "flying saucer," a sphere or a cigar-shaped vessel of some kind. But a UFO resembling a three-stepped stairway? I had never heard of such a thing.

Yet, there was no doubt in my mind that I had seen an Unidentified Flying Object. At the time there was no Internet. The only way in which you could learn more about the subject was to read books or seek the opinion of a friendly UFO enthusiast. That's exactly what I did, but no one seemed to know what it was that I had seen. The mysterious steps in the sky didn't seem to have any possible rational explanation, and for years I carried with me the memory of that absolutely impossible sight.

Things became clearer during the first Iraq war in the early 1990s. At that time, it became known that the U.S. Air Force had developed a revolutionary "invisible" aircraft called the *Nighthawk*. It was the first plane with stealth technology that could render the craft invisible to radar. It all depended on the particular shape of the fighter, a shape that quickly became an icon of modern aeronautic design.

The plane had a sharp line and a flat body, united in a solid block with the wings in order to create a sort of a triangular-shaped body, with the tail also ending in a wedge. That particular shape was able to offer a radar surface of 0.003 meters, similar to that of a swallow, and it helped the fighter to escape radar detection.

When I saw a photograph of the *Nighthawk*, everything fell into place. At last, I had solved the mystery of the stairway to heaven.

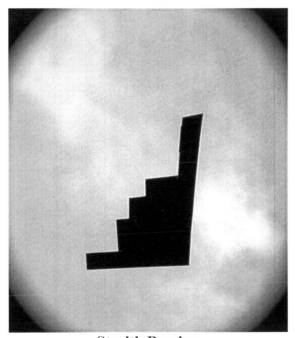

Stealth Bomber
(Photo: Massimo Polidoro)

If you view the plane from directly below, it looks exactly like a stairway with three steps. If you see it backlight by the sun, like I had, it appears to be black although it is difficult to discern any details of the craft. Finally, the impression that it was standing still was an illusion due to the fact that I saw the plane as it was turning around and, when it turned on its axis, the effect was for it to appear smaller and smaller. Its final disappearance, without a trace, was because it was a subsonic plane with two turbo fans and no afterburner—meaning the craft left no vapor trails.

But there was one final piece of the puzzle that needed to be put in place. How plausible was it for an American stealth combat airplane to fly above Pordenone, Italy? The answer is: Very likely, since there was (and still is) a NATO base in nearby Aviano that is managed by the U.S. Air Force. There is no doubt that in the early 1980s, after the invention of this craft, military exercises were taking place in the sky above Pordenone.

This experience showed me how it was possible for rational, sober people to be convinced, in perfectly good faith, that they had witnessed a UFO. When I saw my UFO, an alternative explanation existed, but that information was not yet available to the public. Had I not learned about the existence of stealth planes, I might still be wondering what that little stairway in the sky had been. And who knows how many other military experiments have taken place above our heads. We will probably never know…

Being able to finally solve this mystery paved the way for me to look into other mysterious experiences and I became interested in investigating the paranormal.

All The Right Noises

The very first investigation I conducted took place in January 1989, right after the foundation of CICAP, the Italian skeptics organization. It was a case of a poltergeist.

"Poltergeist" is a German word that means "noisy spirit." It is believed that poltergeists make their presence known by throwing objects around, making rapping sounds, starting fires or by producing electrical disturbances.

The media had devoted a lot of attention to the strange case of Marco, a 12-year-old boy living with his parents in Milano. He seemed to be at the center of some very mysterious activity: Furniture moving around the house, pictures falling off the walls, and books flying across the room. An exorcist was called in to assist, and also a psychic healer, a medium and several parapsychologists, although no one was able to restore peace to the home.

Since the birth of CICAP had attracted some media attention just a few weeks before, several journalists immediately called upon us to investigate the case. However, it was only when the family themselves called us in distress that we decided to step in to help.

We met with Marco's family and decided on the following procedure: A few colleagues would talk with his parents to gather an account of the events and outline their psychological profile, while I would spend time with Marco, allowing him to play with his toys as I tried to understand what was going on.

We spent three days with Marco and his family. Nothing supernatural occurred during our time there, although several interesting facts came to light. First of all, the family appeared to be very open to psychic phenomena as there were many books about supernatural topics sitting on their shelves. Marco had watched several movies that may have influenced him, such as *Poltergeist, The Exorcist,* and *A Nightmare on Elm Street.* His parents attended séances, and consulted palm readers and other psychics. Furthermore, there appeared to be some tension within the family because the parents' work commitments conflicted with their son's needs for their attention.

What appeared to be most revealing, however, was the fact that some members of the family had, on several occasions, caught Marco in the act of throwing objects around the house.

"Oh, but that was nothing!" dismissed his parents. "Those few times he was only playing, but on every other occasion the phenomena were real."

"What other occasions?" we asked. "Did anyone ever see a book take flight or a frame fall off the wall?"

Well, it appeared that nobody, except Marco, had ever witnessed any poltergeist phenomena. At most, somebody had seen an object after it had hit the ground, and only because Marco had yelled to attract attention. Usually, the phenomena only took place in the presence of Marco, especially when he was alone in the room...

Those three days I spent with Marco showed me that he was an intelligent boy, with a good sense of humor, but he was also very alert in watching all of my movements. I was careful to never let him go unobserved. Strangely, nothing paranormal happened in our presence. Marco's parents told us clearly that those were the first three days that had been totally devoid of phenomena. They could not explain why this was so. Had the poltergeist simply run its course?

On our last day there, however, something did happen.

I wanted to see whether, if given the opportunity, Marco would seize it and try to trick us. So I relaxed my attention on him. I let him play and frequently turned my back to him. At one point during the evening, while we played a computer game, he suggested that I continue playing while he prepared his books for school the following day.

"I can help you," I offered.

"No, no!" he insisted. "Please keep on playing. I'll be done soon."

I turned back to the game but managed to keep an eye on Marco through his reflection in a window. I watched him place some books into his bag, as he looked back at me frequently. Then, he took an object out of his bag and in a sudden movement he threw it against a wall. It turned out to be a glass and it shattered with a loud "BANG!"

I'd caught him red-handed.

I immediately turned around.

"Why did you do that?" I asked him.

He looked puzzled.

"What do you mean?"

"I was watching your reflection," I explained. "Why did you throw that glass at the wall?"

"I… I…" he stuttered.

Marco couldn't finish his sentence, however, because his father appeared in the room in excitement.

"Did it finally happen?" he asked. "Did the poltergeist throw something? You witnessed it, right?"

"No," I replied. "I clumsily knocked over a glass and smashed it."

"Oh, that's all?" he asked in frustration.

"Yes. I am very sorry."

The kid didn't look me in the eye, but continued putting his books away in his bag, in silence. I invented that excuse because I didn't want to embarrass him in front of his father.

We concluded that Marco was a normal kid who just needed more attention from his parents and who discovered, one day, that if he threw things around while nobody could see him that he would suddenly get a lot of attention. Not only attention from his parents but also from the media and a number of strange and funny people who came to visit him. When I played with him and his toys he couldn't care less about psychic phenomena and poltergeists and, not so mysteriously, nothing paranormal happened. Only when we announced that we were leaving did Marco cause something to happen. Why did he do it? Was it because he didn't want his family to be seen as liars? Or did he do it because he didn't want us to leave? I don't think I'll ever know the answers to these questions.

However, I do know that from the day we left, the mysterious activity ceased.

Massimo Polidoro is an investigator of the paranormal, a writer, lecturer, and head of CICAP, the Italian skeptics group. During the past 25 years, Massimo has investigated hundreds of cases of paranormal events and historical enigmas. He has conducted many investigations at haunted castles and cemeteries, walked on hot-coals, examined poltergeist manifestations and recreated crop circles. He has also tested psychics, mediums, human magnets, girls with X-ray eyes, table-tippers, prophets, healers, and many others. He is the author of over 40 books including *Secrets of the Psychics: Investigating Paranormal Claims* and *Final Séance: The Strange Friendship Between Houdini and Doyle*. Massimo is currently working on the biography of his mentor, James "The Amazing" Randi. www.massimopolidoro.com.

Area 51: What Is Really Going On In There?

Donald R. Prothero

We are sneaking in through the back door to the infamous Area 51.

We drive west across the Nevada State Highway 375, better known as the "Extraterrestrial Highway," about three hours north from Las Vegas. The road itself is unremarkable—miles and miles of a ribbon of asphalt cutting across barren desert of mesquite and Joshua tree yuccas. No signs of life anywhere. Occasionally the road rises up from the low flats to cross a small mountain range, with jagged rocks exposed on all sides, completely devoid of vegetation. During the summer, the temperatures stay above 100°F for weeks on end, and almost no one comes through here. In the winter, the daytime temperatures are more comfortable, but at night it gets bitterly cold, especially if the desert winds are howling through the area. We're also over 4400 feet in elevation, and some winters are cold enough that snow accumulates on the high desert surface, and may persist on the peaks well into the spring.

After you pass through the tiny towns of Alamo and Ash Springs (the last gas station for 150 miles or more) on U.S. Highway 93, and turn west onto the Extraterrestrial Highway, you drive about 15 miles until you reach Hancock Summit, a mountain pass over barren rock that is the highest place in the region. You can get out of your car and look to the southwest, but all you will see is the Groom Range to your west. Area 51 is down in the valley beyond, and there is no other spot in any direction where you could see the base from the paved road. You can make the strenuous hike to Tikaboo Peak to the south, and see parts of the base on the other side of the range without incurring the wrath of base security, but this isn't much more revealing.

The isolation of the base was deliberate. Its location was purposely chosen to be as remote as possible, and impossible to see from the paved road, no matter how high up you drive. Until recently, the only way to see the base was by airplane, and the entire airspace above the base is restricted. So unless you want to be chased away by fighter jets, you don't try to fly over it with a civilian craft. Then, when spy satellites and Google Earth became available to anyone with a computer, it was possible to get satellite images of the base. But all these show are a series of airstrips and a bunch of buildings down on the valley floor next to the dry Groom Lake bed. Sure, you can see there is military activity there, but this reveals nothing that is worth getting excited over. It looks just like any other desert military airstrip.

Satellite of Groom Lake
(Photo: NASA)

Driving southwest and down from Hancock Summit, you come to a right curve, where the paved highway veers off to the northwest. Going straight ahead is Groom Lake Road, the primary entrance to the base, deliberately left unpaved and unmarked and hard to find, so only authorized people will drive this way. If you veer off down this dusty road, there are sensors underneath that will let them know you're coming. After about 13 miles, you come to the first signs that warn you this is a closed military installation, and that photography is not permitted. Meanwhile, on the hills above the road are several lookout spots where the "Camo dudes" (as some people call the security personnel) are watching you with high-powered binoculars from their white Jeep Cherokees or Chevy pickup trucks. If you stop and look around, you'll see not only their vehicles, but also security cameras on posts. Finally, at 13.8 miles from the unmarked turnoff from Highway

375, the last sign informs you that you are on the base perimeter, photography is not permitted, do not go any further, and, by the way, the use of deadly force is authorized. These folks aren't kidding! The perimeter is marked not by a big fence, but by a series of large orange posts spaced about 50 yards apart on the base borderline. As long as you stay in your vehicle and don't cross the line, you'll probably be okay. Lately, they have even begun to tolerate photography of the signs and the base perimeter. But if you drive past the signs, or get out and walk too close to the line of posts, they will swoop down, arrest you, and turn you over to the Lincoln County Sheriff, to whom you will have to pay a steep fine for trespassing on a restricted military base.

If you were allowed to pass this perimeter fence, you would drive another 0.8 miles through a canyon between the mountains before you even get to the actual guard post. Tourists and casual UFO fans never get this far, because the checkpoint is well inside the restricted area. If you're driving on the road at 4:40 p.m. during the working week, you need to pull over onto the shoulder to let the big white bus speeding out of the base pass you as it transports out authorized personnel.

Hikers try to sneak inside the base perimeter and take photographs from the mountains that overlook Groom Lake, but most are caught quickly before they ever get there. If you are lucky and stick around long enough, you'll see the Pave Hawk security helicopters swoop overhead, watching for hikers trying to pussyfoot past the perimeter. At one time, these choppers swooped down low and "sandblasted" trespassers with the downwash from their rotors to drive them back and discourage them, but that practice is no longer allowed.

Driving past the unmarked entrance to Groom Lake Road, about 5 miles further to the northwest on Highway 375, there's a small mailbox by the side of the wide graveled parking area south of the main highway. This is the legendary "black mailbox" that is so popular in the lore of UFO fans. Oddly, it's not colored black at all, but a dull dirty white, and it has so many stickers from all over the world and so much graffiti scrawled on it that the color is obscured. The "black" refers to the original mailbox that was here before 1996, a regular black-painted county mailbox you could buy in a local hardware store. Despite all the legends, the truth is much less glamorous. It's not even a mailbox for the base! Naturally, the military has its own system for delivering mail, and would never use a mailbox accessible to the public. Instead, it's the mailbox for the only rancher in this area of the Tikaboo Valley. He has to cope with the constant problem of UFO fans breaking his mailbox open, searching his mail looking for "top-secret military posts," and even shooting at it. The original mailbox was eventually removed and auctioned off to a UFO fan for $1000. Its replacement is tightly padlocked and bulletproof, so the only thing tourists can do is decorate its outside. But this area around the mailbox is a favorite place for UFO fans to hang out at nighttime, and even camp overnight, trying to get a glimpse of anything flying in the skies.

The "Black" Mailbox
(Photo: D.R. Prothero)

So be forewarned: Curious UFO tourists can wander around the perimeter and get their thrills approaching the various entrances to Area 51, but if you cross the line, you'll be sorry!

In the past few decades, this perfectly ordinary military base in the middle of the desert in southern Nevada has taken on mythical status. Most military bases have tight security, and only authorized military personnel and their contractors are allowed on base. This particular base is top secret, with much tighter security than most military land. Not only is it surrounded by a secured perimeter and motion detectors in the ground, but guards patrol the perimeter regularly, and have video security cameras monitoring anything that comes near the fence. It is also located in one of the most remote areas of Nevada, which is more than two hours drive north of Las Vegas. Naturally, the high level of secrecy surrounding the base has led to all sorts of speculation about what happens there. An entire industry of books, movies and TV shows need only mention "Area 51" and immediately their audience assume that there are aliens or some kind of weird government experiments going on there.

For many decades, the activities in the base were top secret, so most of what was written about it was sheer guesswork or based on the reports of people who had worked there and spilled some of their information. The mystery only helped spur on a lot of baseless gossip, especially by those who assumed that UFOs must be involved if the government was hiding their activities so strenuously. But in July 2013, in response to a Freedom of Information Act request, the CIA released nearly all the documentation about Area 51 and its activities, and nearly all of the past work on the "Dreamland Resort" (an old code name for the base that concealed its real purpose) has been revealed. This documentation, along with the interviews of veterans of those projects compiled in recent books, dispels much of the mythology that had grown up around the base.

In 1955, the CIA asked the Atomic Energy Commission to add the land to its existing grid from the Atomic Test Site, and the designation "Area 51" came to be official. Shortly thereafter, original airstrip, trailer homes, and a few shacks that were used during World War II were transformed into a much bigger base. In the months that followed, the base expanded to include a long paved runway with three hangars and a control tower, plus accommodations for the Lockheed and CIA personnel working on the base, including a movie theater, mess hall, trailer homes, a water tower and fuel tanks. Soon there were regular flights bringing Lockheed personnel and supplies up from Burbank, California, where Lockheed's main plant was located. These shuttle flights are now known as the "Janet" flights. Passengers dressed to be inconspicuous board these Janet flights daily at Las

Vegas' McCarran Airport, and are given special Air Traffic Control priority.

My father, Clifford Ross Prothero, worked for Lockheed Aircraft his entire career. Originally trained as an artist, he started out building the legendary P-38 fighter plane during World War II, and then he became one of the founding members of the Technical Illustration department. During the 1950s–60s, when he carried a top-security clearance badge, he told us that he could say nothing about where he was working or what he was doing. Most of the time, he came back home very late each night, but I remember many times where he was gone all week, and my mother was not allowed to tell us where he went. Only after he retired did he tell me about those long flights out to Area 51.

Lockheed's U-2 (which my dad worked on) was developed by engineers at the Skunk Works in the early 1950s, and first flown in 1955 at Area 51. By 1957 it was in service for the CIA and U.S. Air Force. It was their main high-altitude spy plane, and was top secret until 1960 when a plane was shot down over the Soviet Union, causing an international crisis. Even before this incident, the CIA was seeking a spy plane that could fly higher above the Soviet missile ceiling, and was sturdy enough and fast enough to outrun interceptor planes as well. This effort was further accelerated after the U-2 incident, and the vulnerabilities that the U-2 revealed. This became the CIA's "Project OXCART," the top-secret program to develop the next-generation spy plane, Lockeed's A-12. This evolved into the YF-12, the eventual predecessor of the legendary SR-71 "Blackbird" spy plane, the most successful aircraft of its kind ever built.

Finally, Area 51 played a crucial role in the development and testing of Lockheed's A-117 Nighthawk Stealth Fighter. The plane first saw combat in the Balkan wars of 1999, where one was shot down by a surface-to-air missile, and its secrecy was exposed. The first aircraft into Iraq during the 1991 and 2003 Persian Gulf wars were stealth craft, which were able to evade Iraqi radar as they delivered laser-guided bombs to their targets. Although they had been spotted, the Air Force officially refused to acknowledge the existence of the F-117 until 1988, and in 2008 the Air Force retired the plane because the A-22 Raptors were due to be delivered.

So what about the UFOs and aliens?

The long history of secrecy surrounding Area 51 has led some people to believe that the government was hiding more than top-secret spy and stealth aircraft. Just the fact that the CIA and the military went to such great lengths to conceal what they were doing feeds into these suspicions, and makes the conspiracy-minded more convinced of their beliefs. The popular media (TV shows such as the "X-Files," documentaries about Area 51 on cable TV, and many movies, especially "Independence Day") have created these myths based on what the screenwriters imagine could be going on behind that curtain of secrecy. Screenwriters are only interested in a gripping story that will sell their scripts and hold an audience, so they have no interest in making a movie about the truth; they are only telling a good tale. Their influence on pop culture is overwhelming, so enough people have seen these shows enough times that no amount of revelation of the more mundane explanation will convince them that they are believing a Hollywood fantasy.

In addition to the speculation from the outside world, quite a few members of the high-security staff at Groom Lake were more than happy to let these myths spread. After all, alien and UFO stories work as excellent misdirection if people are thinking about these, instead of the reality of secret stealth aircraft and spy planes. But where do these stories come from?

During the 1950s–1970s, civilian aircraft flew no higher than 40,000 feet (and still don't), and military aircraft only a little higher. This was a time of an unusually large number of UFO reports in the area around southern Nevada. Right after the U-2 began flying there was a huge increase in the number of sightings by civilian pilots, and with over 2850 OXCART A-12 flights alone, there were a lot of high-speed, high-altitude craft flying over the civilian airspace. Not only were these craft top secret, but they were traveling over 2000 miles per hour at over 80,000 to 90,000 feet. All the civilian pilots would have seen is an unusually shaped craft, or possibly only a string of lights on its wings, moving much faster and higher than any plane they've ever seen. Some reports about the "fiery" craft were probably the silvery wings of the U-2 or A-12 reflected in the setting sun. The Air Force's "Project Blue Book" checked a long list of UFO sightings and found that most reports in southern Nevada could be explained by spy planes (although they could not divulge that information at the time.) Veterans of Area 51 who were interviewed later agreed with this assessment. According to sources in Annie Jacobsen's *Area 51: An Uncensored History of America's Top Secret Military Base:*

The shape of OXCART was unprecedented, with its wide, disk-like fuselage designed to carry vast quantities of fuel. Commercial pilots cruising over Nevada at dusk would look up and see the bottom of OXCART whiz by at 2,000-plus mph. The aircraft's titanium body, moving as fast as a bullet, would reflect the sun's rays in a way that could make anyone think UFO.

The light show visible above Area 51, especially in the 1960s-1990s, is explained by the testing of the A-12, the SR-71 Blackbird, and the A-117 Nighthawk. These spy aircraft were designed to fly at nighttime, and they looked strange with the spacing and shape of their lights, and their unusual capabilities of speed and maneuverability. There may have been additional craft not mentioned in the conventional accounts, such as still-classified stealth helicopters (used in the raid to kill Osama bin Laden) and other vertical takeoff and landing craft that handily explain why so many people see mysterious objects at night over the area. No UFOs required.

In the end, the truth about Area 51 turns out to be much more mundane. It was certainly a top-secret installation with lots of projects that the CIA and Air Force did not declassify until 2013. They practiced all sorts of subterfuge to keep people guessing. But now that the CIA has released all the formerly top-secret documents, there is no smoking gun in there to suggest that anything other than spy planes and stealth aircraft were being tested and developed. A huge number of early UFO reports are now explained as high-altitude supersonic planes that civilian pilots did not know about.

So again, what about the UFOs and aliens?

Well, we don't have any UFOs and aliens. What we *do* have is a huge number of declassified CIA documents that lay out what really did happen in Area 51. What we *do* have is retired Area 51 personnel, now released from their vows of secrecy, saying that there were *no* alien craft or bodies being stored there. These men had the highest-possible security clearance, and not one saw any aliens. I asked my dad before he passed away what he thought of the stories, since he had been there in the 1960s. He laughed, and said it was all hokum and myths fostered by people who couldn't accept the idea that the secrecy was all about hiding spy aircraft, not aliens and UFOs.

Dr. Donald Prothero is a paleontologist and geologist who specializes in mammalian paleontology. He is the author or editor of over 30 books, including *Abominable Science: The Origin of Yeti, Nessie, and Other Cryptids; Greenhouse of the Dinosaurs: Evolution, Extinction, and the Future of Our Planet,* and *Catastrophes!: Earthquakes, Tsunamis, Tornadoes, and Other Earth-Shattering Disasters.* www.donaldprothero.com/

The Monster Of Newark

Brian Regal

When I was a kid I saw a monster peering into my bedroom window. This monster even attempted to get into my room. My experience may account for a good bit of my adult behavior, though I'm hoping not. It was 1967 after all, and a lot of people were seeing monsters.

I grew up in a three floor walk-up tenement in Newark, New Jersey. The neighborhood was sometimes called "Down Neck" because of the way it was bordered by the Passaic River, and sometimes called "The Ironbound" because it had been a railroad industrial hub in its heyday. I always preferred "Ironbound" as it sounded tougher.

I shared a bedroom with my older sister. It was a front room off the living room with a window that faced a shopping street called Fleming Avenue. The building was an old one, with iron fire escapes, the kind that Film Noir directors were so enamored of in the 1950s because of the way moonlight shone through. There was an entire row of similar buildings attached to ours along the street with no spaces between them. A guy my dad called "The Mayor" lived a couple of doors down. In the summer time, he'd squeeze his considerable bulk into a lawn chair on the sidewalk and sit there all day, no matter the temperature. As people drove by, they would wave to him and yell, "Yo, Toe-Nay!" He smiled back knowingly while chomping on a cigar.

It was not the sort of neighborhood where cryptids showed up.

However, one night as I fell asleep, the fire escape outside the bedroom began to rattle and shake. I looked up to see a monstrous hairy face peering in the window. It had a deranged look in its gaunt eyes. It looked very big but emaciated as it pulled on the metal stairs of the fire escape mechanism. My sister saw it too, and we screamed in horror at this primordial beast that seemed to be trying to get in to eat us.

The figure darted away just as my father rushed into the room. We pointed to the window and he looked out. He sputtered some ancient expletive under his breath he had learned as a tank driver in the Korean War. Then he turned to us. His angry face instantly turned to one of sympathy and fatherly concern.

"Everything is okay," he said with a smile. "Don't worry."

A night or two later the beast returned. This time I heard a terrible commotion outside. Wearing my Flintstones pajamas I bravely opened the window and looked out just as the monster darted between two parked cars, yelping in pain. It was being pursued by another monster that chased him with what looked suspiciously like a baseball bat.

That was the last time we saw the creature. After that, all seemed to return to normal on Fleming Avenue. There were still monsters running around, but none of them tried to get into my room. It got me thinking. How did such a creature know how to operate a fire escape? How had no one noticed it walking down the street in the middle of the Ironbound? I had seen just such a creature in an episode of "Jonny Quest," so I knew how to recognize it, but what about everybody else? There were plenty of strange things on those streets, of course, but even this thing must have aroused comment. I filed those questions away and continued to dream of being an historian or a writer, or at least a tank driver like Pop.

Then one day, I was in the candy store across the street with my mother. She was buying some household things while I perused the magazine rack.

And I saw it.

There, on the cover of a magazine was a picture of the thing that attacked us. The magazine had a title I found difficult to say, AR-GO-SEE.

"Mom! Mom! That's the thing I saw…"

Just as I blurted that out she grabbed my hand and dragged me towards the door.

"Don't play with the books. Come on, we still have to go to the deli and then to the—"

I didn't hear the rest. I kept looking at the magazine cover.

"But…but!"

I waved and pointed feverishly but ineffectively at the magazine rack and tried to get her to understand. It was no use. The pot-roast and pierogies awaited and there was no way she was going to detour for some foolish magazine that her weird little kid was yammering about.

But I was determined. After a few weeks of saving my pennies I returned to the candy store to get a copy of that magazine. Of course, they were all sold out. I never saw it again.

(Photo: Argosy Magazine)

It wasn't until years later that I learned what mysterious creature had intruded upon our lives. I was told the story at the old *Star-Z Tavern* during a typically drunken family baby christening. It seems a young newlywed who lived in the tenement next-door had grown weary of her husband and began an affair with a wiry bakery truck driver. Beau Brummel was not the smartest loaf in the basket, and waited until her husband entered the front door and started coming up the stairs before making his stealthy withdrawal via the fire escape.

The night we encountered him he had climbed over our balcony to continue down our iron ladder.

My Polish father knew what had happened and that we were never in any danger. However, my Irish grandfather who lived up on the third floor felt that action was required. For several evenings in a row he hid in the darkened street-level glass entry doors, wielding my Louisville Slugger, and waited. His patience was rewarded when a few nights later the hapless lover came scrambling down the fire escape ladder. As the Lothario was about to drop down to the safety of the concrete, gramps stepped out, yelled, "Ya bastid, scare my grandkids will ya!" and swung for the fences with an expertise that would have made the Great Bambino proud.

The bat found the man's shins more than once, and Don Juan fell from the ladder. With shouts of "I'm not a burglar, I'm not a burglar!" he bolted away, limping wounded into the night.

The story passed into the lore of Fleming Avenue, and has been told at every family gathering from then on.

Incidents such as this give useful insight into the formation of myths and legends. Some tales of monsters undoubtedly have their origins in some event that was poorly remembered by those involved. From Grimm's fairy tales, to Jack and the Beanstalk, to the Blemmyae of the Middle Ages, to El Chupacabras, and to Spring Heeled Jack, more than a few fantastical stories began with mundane events expanded out of proportion. This can also teach us about the differences between rural and urban legends. They are a wealth of primary source material.

Without including serial killers, dictators, racist, hatred-filled homophobic misogynists, people who drive Hummers, or those who wear shorts and sandals in the winter, it is difficult to prove the existence of monsters. They are annoyingly elusive and require a good bit of work to find. Often when we do, they turn out to be just as annoyingly prosaic. That, however, is the nature of the monster hunting game: Lots of work to discover it was just a guy climbing down a fire escape in the middle of the night, scaring some kids. It makes the entire enterprise so much more interesting and fun, at least, if you begin with the idea that there probably is no flying devil horse or scaly aquatic beast to be found.

Years later while I was working on my biography of Grover Krantz I was finally able to acquire a copy of the *Argosy* magazine with Ivan Sanderson's article featuring the infamous Patterson-Gimlin film stills that allegedly captured Bigfoot. It seemed different to me as an adult to the way I remembered it as a kid. That's the faulty nature of memory, especially the memory of monsters. We always seem to embellish them beyond the facts of what really happened. As an historian, I have been trained to see past the memories, to analyze the texts, to see the correspondences, and to compare against actual data. This is something the vast majority of monster hunters and cryptozoologists need to do a bit more.

Maybe they were just not lucky enough to grow up in the Ironbound and have a grandfather who was handy with a baseball bat.

Dr. Brian Regal teaches the history of science, technology, and medicine at Kean University. He has never seen a UFO or a spirit orb, nor has he ever witnessed anyone spontaneously combust. He is the author of *Searching for Sasquatch: Crackpots, Eggheads, and Cryptozoology; Pseudoscience: A Critical Encyclopedia,* and *Icons of Evolution.* His latest title is *Satan's Harbinger: The Real Story of the Jersey Devil.*

Dream Lover

Eugenie C. Scott

It's not like my ex-husband was a bad guy. But from the start the marriage was probably not a great idea. We were mismatched in many ways. At 39 to my 20, he was almost twice my age. The experiences shaping me were the 1960s peace, environmental, and civil rights movements, while he was shaped by the labor struggles of the 1940s. My music was rock 'n' roll, while his was 1940s jazz. He had nothing in common with my friends, and I gradually stopped seeing them. I was an upper Midwestern Protestant, while he was a Brooklyn Jew, born of Russian immigrant parents. Our incompatibility had nothing to do with religion: Neither of us believed in God. But I grew up in a Lake Wobegon environment where, if you sliced your hand on the lawnmower blade, you patched it up and finished cutting the grass without comment. He could carry on for hours about a hangnail. Everything was larger-than-life and a big production with Bob, whereas I, true to my background, preferred Scandinavian understatement.

Our backgrounds, our references, and our interactions with the world were different, and for three years I kept convincing myself that everything would be okay with just a change in our environment. Once I graduated from college, things would get better. Once I finished my master's degree, things would get better. Once Bob got away from his bad work situation in Milwaukee, things would get better. But things never got better.

In my early 20s I was teaching at a state college. I was friendly with one of the undergraduate anthropology majors, whom I will call Laurie, and who was a practicing Wiccan. Laurie would make small, inscribed charms out of clay, and fire them in her hibachi. The charms were for luck, or for getting a better job, or even for improving one's love life. You could put these (rather attractive) small tokens in your pocket or string a chain through a perforation to make a necklace. Either way, you could take them with you whenever you needed something extra. I knew people who swore that having one of Laurie's charms in their pocket helped them get a job. When I left Bob, Laurie was one of the people I crashed with until I could find my own place.

Laurie was quiet, sweet, gentle, rather mystical, and very soothing. Given my state of mind, it was good for me to be around someone like that. I had courses to teach, lectures to prepare, students to advise, so even if I was feeling pretty shattered, I couldn't just stop everything to heal. And yeah—the Midwestern Scandinavian tradition of suck-it-up dictates that you show up if people depend on you, regardless of how you feel. Oddly, leaving Bob produced in me simultaneous feelings of elation, freedom, and misery. It was one of the most painful and stressful periods of my life.

I was young, pretty, and newly single, and it didn't take very long before suitors (to use an old-fashioned term that we didn't use even then) began showing up. Many of them I politely held at arm's length. But not all.

Among the ones that I didn't hold off was Ben, a tall, dark, brooding, charismatic professor, who provided a broad, well-muscled shoulder to cry on. It didn't take long before we became lovers. Unfortunately, he was married, and both he and I repeatedly tried to break off the relationship. And repeatedly we would get back together again.

All of this personal turmoil took place in the context of the late 1960s, which in many ways was Woo Central. UFOs, cryptozoology, astrology, psychic phenomena, charms for luck or love—whatever the woo, it was easy to find aficionados. There was a lot of mysticism around too, doubtless augmented by the popularity of mind—and sense—altering drugs. Mystical experiences were discussed matter-of-factly: You didn't have to be a Wiccan to have, or know someone who had had, an unexplained experience. It's no coincidence that CSICOP (the Committee for the Scientific Investigation of Claims of the Paranormal, now the Committee for Skeptical Inquiry) was founded a few years later.

One evening Ben came by the apartment, and once again we tried to break off our relationship. This would be the last time we would make love—there would be a complete break; there were many tears. Later that night after he had left, I had a mystical experience. I felt

Ben's presence in the room, as real as if he actually were there, holding me, as he had done several hours before. I felt his warmth, the feeling of his skin against mine, the sound of his breath in my ear—it was real, although simultaneously I knew that it wasn't. I knew that if I opened my eyes, I'd be alone in my bed. But it felt as real as when he had been there earlier. (And that's all the description you're going to get; this isn't going to be an X-rated chapter!)

Perhaps that's why I cut some slack for believers in pseudoscience. I know how real unreal experiences can seem. The human brain is a complicated organ that is more unreliable than we recognize. A person sincerely (as opposed to opportunistically) believing that they have been abducted by an alien or having a Near Death Experience may describe a sensory experience not different from what they experience in everyday life. They see things, hear sounds, feel touches, and smell odors. We all depend on our senses—and so I don't think it is irrational for people to accept such familiar experiences as being real.

Scientific skeptics are unusual in the degree to which we are willing to suspend sensory evidence in favor of alternate explanations. We would explain my "visitation" by Ben, occurring at the border of sleep, as a hypnopompic hallucination, or perhaps a lucid dream, doubtless influenced by an extremely stressful state of mind. It's a more parsimonious explanation than the idea that my lover psychically returned to make love to me. Skeptics prefer naturalistic explanations, but that's a skill that we must learn. In my experience, most people find it more natural to go with the surface explanation: My lover returned, Joe was abducted by an alien, Ravi saw the Hindu god of the dead at the end of the tunnel of light during his NDE.

Back in the apartment, I awoke feeling confused. Something extraordinary had occurred, yet I hadn't "really" confirmed Ben's presence or absence. I had kept my eyes shut. At that point, I hadn't read the skeptical literature and didn't know about tactile, olfactory, and other sensory hallucinations. All I knew was that something had happened that *felt* as real as anything else in my life, and whatever it was, it was a very meaningful event. Laurie had had a lot more experience with mystical experiences, so it was natural that I would check in with her.

When she woke up I asked her, "Did you notice anything funny last night?"

Laurie smiled her sweet, somewhat mystical smile, and said, "You mean when Ben came back?"

...

That would have been a great ending to this story, but that's not quite how it happened.

What I actually said to Laurie when she got up was, "I think Ben came back last night." I recall her smiling and saying, "Yes, I know."

Which isn't the same story as the first ending. But something else that good skeptics have conditioned themselves to consider is how easy it is to misremember events to reinforce beliefs or opinions, or even to make a better story. I remember at the time being shocked and amazed that Laurie "knew" that Ben had returned. I can't believe that she was deliberately being dishonest; it wasn't her character. But being of a generally mystical mindset, she would be able to easily convince herself that something she heard during the night—or thought she heard—was a psychic visitation by my former lover. I had primed her with the thought, and her individual psychology filled in the rest. How very human! Not everyone thinks in terms of blinded experiments, and I'm not going to fault them for it. For me, the goal is to persuade them of the value of a scientific perspective, which requires understanding and even empathizing with their very natural, very human, unscientific response. I've been there.

Eventually, the pain of my broken marriage subsided, and not too much later I met the man who eventually became my current husband, and with whom I've subsequently spent more than 40 (considerably happier!) years. I was still surrounded by late 1960s woo, but being in a better frame of mind, I found myself less susceptible to paranormal explanations. It would be convenient (and self-serving) to say that I returned to my "normal" scientific world-view, but in truth, it was only gradually that I developed the practice—habit, really—of looking more critically at what Carl Sagan has called "extraordinary claims."

Dr. Eugenie Scott is a physical anthropologist, a former university professor, and the founding Executive Director of the National Center for Science Education, serving from 1987-2014. She now serves on their Advisory Council. Dr. Scott has been a leading researcher and activist in the creationism versus evolution controversy and is the author of *Evolution vs. Creationism* and co-editor of *Not In Our Classrooms: Why Intelligent Design Is Wrong For Our Schools.*

Nothing To Lose Sleep Over

Brian A. Sharpless

When I was invited to write this chapter I thought of a few strange experiences I've had. Like most skeptics I've met (although I don't have hard empirical data on this), I've had my share of anomalous events that appeared to defy a simple, logical explanation. But here are a few I decided not to write about:

My childhood dog howled every time someone mentioned the name of a Hindu God. This was rather peculiar, given that I grew up in a small town in Pennsylvania.

While driving home one night I saw a werewolf (although it was probably just a brown bear with anorexia.)

My friend Tina and I were driving to a restaurant approximately forty-five minutes away when we had a Mulder and Scully "X-Files" moment. In spite of the fact that there was no traffic on the road and I was driving over the speed limit, the trip took *3 hours*. Neither of us had the subjective sense that it took that long and we were very confused upon noticing the clock. When we reached the restaurant, which had by then closed, we joked that we were "missing time" like the subjects of a Whitley Schreiber book.

Instead, I thought it would be interesting to focus on a strange experience that is, oddly enough, related to my research. But first, a bit of background might help.

I've spent some time studying unusual things. This started when I was a kid, and one of the first books I remember begging my mother to buy was a tiny purple picture book simply titled *Monsters.* I still have it. My library has grown quite a bit since then, and I've amassed a considerable collection of books dealing with some of the peculiar vicissitudes of the human experience, such as cryptids, UFOs, demonology, and serial killers. At some point, though, I had to "grow up" and research more mainstream things.

I flirted briefly with becoming an archaeologist until I realized that this career path would take me in very different directions than implied by the *Indiana Jones* movies. Disillusioned, but a bit wiser, I chose to study philosophy and clinical psychology at university. I focused specifically on anxiety disorders, trauma, the classification of psychopathology, and 19th century continental philosophy. These are all mainstream and certainly respectable subjects, but I never really lost my attraction to the eccentric and macabre.

After I received my respectable doctorate from Penn State University, I took a respectable post-doctoral research fellowship at the Center for Psychotherapy Research at the University of Pennsylvania. I was involved in respectable projects focused on panic disorder and psychodynamic therapy. In the course of my work I realized that I had an opportunity to study something strange that hadn't received much scientific attention: Sleep paralysis. At that time, sleep paralysis was thought to be especially prevalent in people with panic disorder and in African-Americans. Given that I was living in West Philadelphia and working on a panic disorder grant, this seemed like a winning idea. I quickly created a diagnostic interview and everyone taking part in the study was assessed for this phenomenon.

So you might be wondering, what exactly is sleep paralysis? And why should you care about some esoteric sleep disorder this writer is prattling on about? Sleep paralysis has a very long history of being a naturalistic explanation for supernatural events. Many have argued that sleep paralysis is to blame for the beliefs in witches, demons, vampires, and abductions by fairies. The hallucinatory bestiary of the 21st century has been updated to include more intellectually "palatable" entities such as ghosts, time-traveling shadow people, and technologically advanced aliens with a predilection for orifice probing.

During a typical episode of sleep paralysis you awaken to find yourself conscious and alert, but completely unable to move (hence the "paralysis.") Only your eyes are mobile, while the rest of your body is prone and vulnerable. You may also notice pressure on your chest and difficulty breathing. This has been referred to as "Old Hag Syndrome," from the belief that a witch or 'old hag' sits on the chest of the victims, rendering them immobile. The condition becomes even more uncomfortable if you experience sleep paralysis hallucinations, which are dreams you have while you're awake. These might involve all the senses, including touch. And whereas approximately 30% of dreams are scary, sleep paralysis hallucinations are almost always riddled with fearful imagery. Some sufferers try to scream or cry out for help although they might only be able to squeal, whisper, or whimper.

The reader may also be wondering if I personally suffer from sleep paralysis. Granted, as a number of scholars engage not only in research but also "me-search," this is not an unusual question. Certainly, part of my early interest in anxiety was fueled by chronic neurotic worries and fear of non-being but, in general, the more unusual things I've studied (e.g., sleep paralysis, exploding head syndrome) have been noticeably absent from my psychological makeup. When I'm interviewed about these subjects (as they are the ones I study that inevitably gain the most attention from the general public), reporters ask me if I've experienced it myself. "No," I respond, "But I can't wait until I do!"

After a few years of research, I decided to write a book on the subject with a colleague. This is actually how I met the editor of this book, as I was doing as much promotion as I could to try to get the book out to the general public. I was interviewed for her podcast Monster Talk along with host Blake Smith. I can still vividly recall conducting the interview via Skype in a cheap motel room in Seattle and drinking a Belhaven ale while waiting to fly out to the U.K. to talk about sleep disorders. Another pertinent detail is that *The Nightmare*, Rodney Ascher's documentary horror film on sleep paralysis, was released while I was in England. My publishers thought it would be a good cross-promotion to have me write a review on the movie.

More on this shortly...

I gave the talks, had some fun in London, and saw picturesque castles in northern Yorkshire with my girlfriend. Although we wanted more time there, we eventually had to face the reality of returning to the States via a long plane ride from Heathrow to Seattle. We had a layover in Iceland and, lucky for us, we had enough time to purchase several mini bottles of Brennivin and Birkir at Duty Free to make the flight a little less painful. Those Icelanders make some very unique liqueurs, but I digress... After de-planing, we had a five-hour drive back home. Needless to say, between the plane ride, the car ride, and the 8-hour time difference-induced jetlag, we needed to unwind.

Our brilliant idea for relaxation was to open up a bottle of red wine (yes, even more alcohol), eat one of my delicious homemade pizzas, and screen *The Nightmare* on the home theater. It's a very good movie I've watched several times, but I hope Mr. Ascher will not be offended when I disclose that the combination of the wine and jet-lag made us start to nod off half-way through the film. So, believing discretion to be the better part of valor, we retired for the evening at the very late hour of 8pm. Though normally a notorious insomniac, for once, I slept the sleep of the truly innocent (i.e., the angelic sleep of puppies and baby hedgehogs) until 4am.

I awoke to a very dark room. As I haven't had to sleep with a nightlight on in quite some time (at least since I turned 32), the darkness wasn't particularly noteworthy or scary. However, I noticed something very peculiar. My door opened ever so slightly, and light streamed in from the hallway window. Then, as if being gently nudged by a summer breeze, the door continued to push slowly open. "That's odd," I said to my quasi-dozing self. Then things took an even weirder turn. The shadows in the hallway began to coalesce and I detected movement out of the corner of my eye. I tried to turn my head, but I could not move. With my eyes straining to look downward and to the left, I saw a shadowy head with no discernible features, except for glowing red eyes. No mouth or ears were visible, and it was almost like the character Snake Eyes from the *GI Joe* cartoons. The head moved further inside the room, and I noticed that it was held up by a long, similarly black and serpentine neck. It was like some sort of satanic giraffe-ninja hybrid. I won't overplay my bravery, as I must admit that I experienced a significant rush of fear and dread for what might happen next. However, I quickly realized what was transpiring and said to myself (in my head, of course, as I couldn't speak), "Oh my god, I'm having sleep paralysis!" I watched the malevolent silhouette with interest for a few more seconds, but it suddenly dissipated when my movement returned. I rolled over, as I usually do when I awaken early, to see my girlfriend sleeping with a depth of intensity that only an extinction-level meteor impact could disturb. As one might imagine, this is usually a very annoying experience for a sleep-challenged person, so I decided to get up and take my green-eyed self downstairs for an early morning workout.

An hour later she came down the steps while I was drinking my chalky protein shake and I told her, "I can't believe it, but I FINALLY had sleep paralysis." She replied, "That's really weird… I had it too!" My mind immediately flashed to the alarming possibility that she might have seen the same evil giraffe Slenderman and that there might be something to this shadow person nonsense after all. Alas, she had not. From what I was told, she awoke once in the middle of the night and wanted to hug me, but was unable to move. In a much less excited manner than me, she just asked herself, "Is this sleep paralysis?" before returning to blissful sleep in that annoying manner that she does.

So, two people who had never experienced sleep paralysis in their lives experienced it in the same night and in the same bed. What were we to make of this? The easiest thing in the world would be to crowbar an extra layer of meaning into these events (i.e., believing we were somehow bewitched, that there is some teleological order to the universe, some sense of "fate" or "mystical connection," or maybe believe that I was indeed visited by an entity with paralytic powers who can also appear and disappear at will.) But out of all the possible events that happen every single day to every single person in the world, some of those are bound to seem weird. As anyone who does statistics knows, chance can occasionally be "lumpy." Plus, as a good bit of research demonstrates, my girlfriend and I had set the stage perfectly for sleep paralysis. We were jetlagged, sleep-deprived, tired, and drinking alcohol. Alcohol acts as a suppressor of REM sleep, making you more likely to have intense dream activity as the night goes on. There's also the very real possibility that the power of suggestion was at play following our film screening. After all, some of the earliest writings on sleep paralysis have noted that it can be "contagious."

So, whereas having a sleep paralysis episode, seeing a shadow person, and having my girlfriend experience an episode during the same night is nowhere near as dramatic as escaping from a Wendigo in the North Woods or being nocturnally abducted by an alien space craft, these strange events nonetheless left me puzzled and confused. For a moment at least, my hallucinations seemed real and I feared for my safety.

After all, I know that that satanic giraffe-ninja was up to no good.

Dr. Brian Sharpless is an Associate Professor of Clinical Psychology at the American School of Professional Psychology at Argosy University, Washington D.C. He has published widely on common and lesser-known psychological disorders, psychodynamic therapy, cognitive-behavioral therapy, professional issues, and the history/philosophy of clinical psychology. His first book, *Sleep Paralysis: Historical Psychological, and Medical Perspectives*, co-authored with Dr. Karl Doghramji, was recently released by Oxford University Press. His first edited book with the same press, *Unusual and Rare Psychological Disorders: A Handbook for Clinical Practice and Research*, was just released. Dr. Sharpless has presented his work at national and international professional conferences and been interviewed for various TV, radio, and print outlets, including National Geographic, *Huffington Post, New York Magazine*, and the BBC.

Hitting The Brakes On Time

Steve Shaw (Banachek)

The year was 1972. The place was Port Elizabeth, South Africa. Our destination was the drive-in movie theater near the Marist Brothers College where I would go to school for a year and play rugby and water polo; two sports I was not great at. Soccer was to be my thing.

At the time, my stepfather Tom Martin was driving. (Yes, that means my name was Steve Martin back before the name became famous for a comedian/actor who also does magic.) I sat in the passenger seat, with my younger brothers David and Barry in the back.

Tom had a huge car, built like a tank, but I am going to guess that most Americans have not heard of the make. It was a gray Wolseley, built by the British manufacturer Wolseley Motors Limited. My stepfather once drove the car straight into a stone wall. The wall was destroyed even though it was made of large boulders backed by dirt and a huge tree, while the Wolseley had nary a scratch.

The Wolseley was considered the finest "area car" ever employed by the London Metropolitan Police. This car had a top speed of 97.6 miles per hour and went from 0 to 60 in 14.4 seconds. I mention this speed and the fact my stepfather fitted the car with Lockheed drum breaks at the rear for a reason. The first week we arrived in Port Elizabeth, after a long train ride from Johannesburg, my stepfather drove the car head on towards me and then hit the breaks suddenly, to show me that "they worked." I was scared shitless, but I digress.

On our way to the movies, we drove down a steep street that is now known as the William Motley Expressway. We were somewhere between Lily Street and Main Street when something happened that I will remember until the day I die.

I can still see the incident clearly. Ahead of us, a man was walking on the sidewalk to our right. He started to step out onto the road. My stepfather slowed down, but the man stepped back onto the curb, so Tom sped back up again. Then, for no apparent reason, the man leapt out into the middle of the road.

There was no time to swerve or slow down. But at that moment, my very sense of time hit the brakes. In slow motion, I watched the man hit the front of the car and fly high into the air. For what seemed like minutes, our car swung around until we came to a bumpy stop. We had rotated 180 degrees and I watched the man fall from the air slowly and land on the ground.

My youngest brother Barry cried out, "Daddy hit a native!" Keep in mind the context of apartheid at the time. "Native" was a very nice description of a black man compared to the horrible labels white Afrikaners used back then. Apartheid was horrific. And at some future time I might write of my experiences of being an English boy in South Africa and not understanding why white Afrikaners treated black people the way they did. But that is a story for another time.

Unable to move any faster, I opened the car door at a snail's pace. I looked down at my clothes and in the twilight I thought I was covered in oil, but upon closer inspection I saw that it was blood. Slowly I turned to look at the man, lying in the road. I realized in horror that one of his legs was hanging off. Some passersby came over to help and wrapped the man's leg in newspapers while we waited for the ambulance to arrive.

Eventually, the scene around me crept up to the regular passage of time as I normally knew it. But during the accident, time had slowed. Even now I can see the man's shoe float into the air and then hover above our car as if it were levitating.

The man was taken to the hospital. A few weeks later when the police came to our home to follow up about the accident, we asked about his condition. The police admitted they had lost track of him. How does that happen? Tragically, during apartheid, it happened a lot. In those days, black lives simply did not matter to the white Afrikaner.

This was not the first occasion that time slowed down for me, but it was the most dramatic. I could see every single detail of the event as if each second had been stretched into minutes.

This brings me to a more recent incident that occurred in Las Vegas, the city in which I currently live. In June 2016, I was driving down a back street when I paused at a stop sign. There was a wall to my right and I could only see part way down the road. The street in that direction appeared clear, so I proceeded to cross slowly. I checked to my left, which was also empty. By the time I looked back to my right side again a blue Nissan Pathfinder was merely yards away, heading full speed towards my truck.

Time seemed to slow down again, not as much as during the accident in South Africa, but enough for my brain to go into overdrive. I knew—at the speed he was traveling—that he was going to hit the front of my vehicle, and if he did I would most likely die. So, instead of hitting the breaks, I hit the gas pedal. He slammed into the side panel of my truck, between the front and rear passenger doors, which happens to be the strongest part of the vehicle. Had I not reacted the way I did I probably wouldn't be telling this story now.

In this case, once the collision occurred, everything immediately went back to regular speed.

The accompanying photo hardly does justice to the damage sustained by my truck. The side where I was hit was rammed in by at least a foot. But here is the interesting thing—other than the fact that both of us walked away from the wreck—I remember each and every thought that came to me as if it was happening in slow motion. I recall every detail vividly, seeing the horrified expression on his face as he knew the inevitable was about to happen; seeing him come towards me, fast at first, and then slowly enough to allow me to react quickly and make decisions that saved my life.

(Photo: Steve Shaw)

I am not the only person who has experienced this quick thinking during an accident. In 1892, geologist Albert von St. Gallen Heim wrote that nearly 95% of climbers, who reported their experiences to him about their accidental falls, had experienced:

"A dominant mental quickness and sense of surety. Mental activity became enormous, rising to a 100-fold velocity or intensity. The relationships of events and their probable outcomes were over-viewed with objective clarity. No confusion entered at all. Time became greatly expanded. The individual acted with lightning-quickness in accord with accurate judgment of his situation." (Noyes and Kletti, 1972, "The experience of dying from falls," *Omega*.)

The same authors also give the example of a jet pilot during the Vietnam War who acted unusually fast and purposefully to save his life when his jet was improperly launched:

"When the nose-wheel strut collapsed I vividly recalled, in a matter of about 3 seconds, over a dozen actions necessary to successful recovery of flight attitude. The procedures I needed were readily available. I had almost total recall and felt in complete control. I seemed to be doing everything that I could and doing it properly." (Noyes and Kletti, 1976, "Depersonalization in the face of life-threatening danger: A description," *Psychiatry*.)

This unusually fast speed appears to be a normal reaction for people when they believe they are in a potentially fatal situation, and so is the perception that time has slowed down during the event. Valtteri Arstilia writes:

"The experienced speed of the passage of time is not constant as time can seem to fly or slow down depending on the circumstances we are in. Anecdotally, accidents and other frightening events are extreme examples of the latter; people who have survived accidents often report altered phenomenology including how everything appeared to happen in slow motion." ("Time Slows Down During Accidents," *Frontiers in Psychology*, 27 June 2012.)

For people who have experienced sudden life-threatening situations, Arstilia observes the following features:

1. The feeling of time expanding and slowing down to a great extent.

2. Dominant mental quickness as demonstrated by the increased speed of thoughts.

3. An altered sense of the duration of the event lasting longer than it actually does.

4. Actions of the experiencer becoming fast and purposeful.

5. An altered and narrow focus on the issues relevant for survival.

6. Unusually sharp vision or hearing.

So, what's going on in these cases?

Arstilia says that, as time in the real world does not really slow down during accidents, it is our internal processes that are somehow altered. There are two things going on here. First, he attributes our unusually fast reactions in these situations to the increased activity of the brain's locus coeruleus norepinephrine system. Second, the experience of time slowing down results from the fact that the relation between the temporal properties of events in the external world and internal states is suddenly distorted due to the increased speed of our internal processes. The phenomenon is part of a fight-or-flight response that is triggered by a perception of a fearful and threatening situation.

All I know is that it is indeed a real phenomenon, internal or not. I also realize that the older I get, the less time seems to stand still. Now we do know the reason for this, or at least scientists say they do. It seems that as we get older we lay down less memory tracks since our brains have already "been there and done that." When one is laying down new tracks, time slows. Time often seems expanded when we focus upon certain tasks. Look at a clock and watch the second hand, it will appear that time has slowed if you concentrate on each and every second compared to just sitting back and letting a minute tick by.

Most of the time we experience in our lives, especially as we get older, is only perceived time. And during those moments when time itself appears to hit the brakes, we think fast, we react fast, and we are seemingly superhuman. Maybe this is a real kind of magic. It is certainly the superpower I would want if I could have one: The power to make time stand still.

Steve Shaw (Banachek) is the world's leading mindreader. He is a magic consultant for Criss Angel, Penn & Teller, David Blaine and Lance Burton, and he invents magic and mentalist effects, including the famous bullet catch trick and the buried alive stunt. Having astounded audiences across the globe, his talents are so incredible that he is the only mentalist ever to fool scientists into believing he possessed psychic powers, and then later reveal he was fooling them. He is a star of the stage act *The Supernaturalists* and he appears on the TV show *Mindfreak*. Banachek is also the author of several books, including *Psychophysiological Thought Reading* and *Psychological Subtleties 2*. www.banachek.com

Identified Flying Objects

Robert Sheaffer

I'm a skeptic when it comes to UFOs, but I've seen quite a few of them over the years.

The first time I saw a UFO was in Chicago in the 1950s. It was late one summer evening around Labor Day when I was about twelve. I was standing in my driveway with a friend. We leaned back lazily against my parent's car and chatted, as we looked upward towards the sky. Suddenly, we saw what appeared to be three disc-shaped objects flying over us in a V-shaped formation. They glowed as they glided smoothly and silently by. We stared in amazement. As the objects approached the horizon, they seemed to disappear.

We thought we had seen something extraordinary.

At that time the whole country was in the midst of a UFO craze. This was soon after the first famous UFO sighting in 1947, when pilot Kenneth Arnold saw a group of objects while flying his small plane near Mount Rainier in Washington. Arnold reported that the objects were shaped like "discs" or "pie plates" and they "moved like saucers skipping across the water." The newspapers dubbed them "flying saucers" and the name stuck. Within a few weeks a wave of saucer sightings spread across the United States, and soon across the world. This led to fears of a government cover-up; a simple conspiracy theory along the lines of, "The Air Force knows more about the flying saucers than they are telling us."

There was also a fascination with Mars. Early scientists believed the planet was covered with crisscrossing canals, which must have been built by intelligent living beings. Books and movies told of humanoid Martians with telepathic abilities that were going to invade earth, kidnap humans and take them back to Mars. In September 1956 there was a very close approach of Mars to Earth. I remember going outside with my father to look for it. As we stared into the night sky he pointed to a light and said, "See that bright red object? That's Mars."

From that point on I was fascinated by astronomy, so my parents bought me a telescope. It was a 3-inch reflector with a really crummy eyepiece, and on top of that, we lived just outside Chicago where the skies never got dark. But I didn't let that stop me, as I eagerly looked at Jupiter, Saturn, and the moon. I couldn't see much else! Later my father helped me to build a much bigger 6-inch telescope made from spare parts. I could see a great deal more with that one.

And it was with this telescope that I saw another UFO.

I was in the backyard with a friend. Using my new telescope we saw what appeared to be the NASA Echo 1 satellite. This satellite, a giant inflated balloon, was the brightest object in Earth's orbit in the early 1960s, and people used to watch it pass overhead. But this time it seemed to be going off course. It zigzagged, veering from left to right and back again. Surely a real satellite wouldn't behave like that, we thought. It must be one of those things that the Air Force doesn't want to tell us about!

After high school, I enrolled at Northwestern University in Evanston, Illinois, majoring in mathematics. I also took courses in astronomy. Dr. J. Allen Hynek, who also happened to be a leading proponent of UFOs, taught some of these classes. He was the guy who came up with the phrase "close encounters of the third kind" and he even made a cameo appearance in the Steven Spielberg movie of the same name. Hynek became a friend, although the more I learned about astronomy and science, the more I realized that it was unlikely I had seen "real" flying saucers. I still believed I had seen something strange, I just didn't know what. It wasn't until years later that I saw the mysterious glowing, smoothly gliding objects again—but on this occasion I had enough time to figure out exactly what they were.

Birds.

They were low flying migratory birds, headed south at the end of summer.

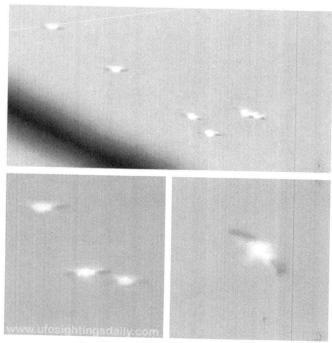

A fleet of UFOs or a flock of birds?
(Photo: UFO Sightings Daily)

This kind of mistake is not unusual. In 1951, three professors at Texas Technical College witnessed an unusual formation of lights over the city of Lubbock. As reported in the *UFO Casebook*, the witnesses saw:

> "A number of lights race noiselessly across the sky, from horizon to horizon, in a few seconds. They gave the impression of about 30 luminous beads, arranged in a crescent shape. A few moments later another similar formation flashed across the night. This time the scientists were able to judge that the lights moved through 30 degrees of arc in a second."

This incident, known as the Lubbock Lights, is now regarded as one of the first great UFO cases. However, several of the witnesses later concluded that they had probably just seen a flock of migrating birds.

What about our sighting of the satellite that seemed to zigzag? Well, we had probably made a mistake in our observation. As I later learned, human perception and memory can be unreliable. Seven years before he would become president of the U.S., Jimmy Carter saw a UFO. One night in October 1969 he had seen a strange object in the western skies of Georgia. It was a disc-shaped light "as bright as the moon" that approached, changed color from white to blue and red, and then retreated into the distance. When he made an official report of his sighting with the International UFO Bureau it was several years after the incident. I examined the report and discovered that, because Carter had been about to give a speech at a Lion's Club that evening, the sighting had occurred in January, not October. I also consulted a star chart and was able to establish that Venus was in the precise location described by Carter. The soon-to-be President hadn't seen an alien spacecraft—he'd probably misidentified the planet Venus.

The eyewitness testimony of even a future president of the United States cannot be taken at face value when investigating UFO sightings. But Mr. Carter is in good company if he did misidentify Venus as a UFO. Many highly trained and responsible people, including airplane pilots, scientists, police officers, and military personnel, have made the same mistake. During World War II, U.S. aircraft tried to shoot down Venus on numerous occasions, believing it to be an enemy aircraft.

By the 1960s, the phrase "flying saucers" had fallen out of fashion and been replaced by "UFO"—or Unidentified Flying Object—a term coined by the U.S. Air Force. UFO refers to *any* unexplained aerial phenomena, although the term is still synonymous with alien spacecraft.

So, what are UFOs?

As the name suggests, UFOs are unidentified objects seen in the skies. But in no way does this mean that the objects are *unidentifiable*. Just as my first UFO sighting and the Lubbock Lights can be explained as birds, many UFOs *have* been identified. When we find an explanation for a UFO it becomes an Identified Flying Object. Of course, each UFO is different and we need to examine individual cases before we can determine precisely what was seen. Having said that, the majority of UFOs can be explained as sightings of natural phenomena, such as clouds and meteors, or human made objects, like aircraft, weather balloons, and satellites.

Witnesses, no matter how credible, can make mistakes in their reporting—we're only human. Optical illusions and reflections can play tricks with our eyes. We can be fooled by atmospheric anomalies that we haven't seen before, such as sundogs and shooting stars. Other humans can also try to fool us. Many UFO sightings have turned out to be hoaxes. Hoaxers make false reports and create fake UFOs using hubcaps, Frisbees, pie tins, and dustbin lids. Photos of UFOs are often as blurry as photos of Bigfoot, and many examples are altered with image editing software.

One of the most infamous hoaxes was the Hudson Valley sightings in the 1980s, when thousands of people in New York spotted an enormous boomerang-shaped UFO covered with blinking lights. The sightings were eventually traced to the Stormville Flyers; a group of small plane pilots who attached colored lights to their planes and flew in formation. By switching off their lights on cue the ship would disappear mysteriously.

Some UFOs remain unexplained. But does this mean these ones are alien spacecraft? Well, no. But that doesn't mean we should end our search for extraterrestrial intelligence. We have explored our own solar system well enough to know that it probably doesn't contain any other advanced civilization like our own. So now we should take that exciting yet terrifying plunge into the depths of interstellar space to continue our search. It is entirely possible that our galaxy may possess many intelligent civilizations. In particular, the possibility of discovering and communicating with other intelligent civilizations using electromagnetic waves offers us some hope of overcoming our own galactic isolation.

And so I keep looking up into the skies.

Robert Sheaffer is one of the world's leading investigators of UFOs. He is a freelance writer whose articles have appeared in *OMNI, Scientific American, Spaceflight, Astronomy, The Humanist, Free Inquiry,* and *Reason,* and he is a regular columnist for *Skeptical Inquirer.* He is the author of *The UFO Verdict: Examining the Evidence, UFO Sightings: The Evidence,* and he is a contributor to

Extraterrestrials—Where Are They?, which *Science* magazine called "One of the most interesting and important of the decade. Robert's most recent book is *Bad UFOs*, named after his blog, which covers the latest developments on the UFO scene at www.badufo.com. Robert lives near San Diego, California.

I Saw The Light

Aiden Sinclair

I checked in late the night I stayed at Manresa Castle in Port Townsend, Washington. Exhausted, I dragged myself upstairs to my room, tossed a few personal items on the TV nightstand and crawled straight into bed. I awoke early the next morning and went downstairs to breakfast. When I returned to my room, I noticed that the objects I thought I'd thrown mindlessly onto the nightstand had been moved. My shirt studs had been lined up carefully, while a handful of coins were arranged according to denomination. I had only been out of the room for about half an hour and no one else had been in the room while I was gone.

Shirt Studs and Coins
(Photo: Aiden Sinclair)

I later discovered that a friend of mine had stayed at the hotel previously. He was given the exact same room, number 306, where he had a strange experience too. He left his room for dinner and when he retuned, his suitcase had been opened, while several pairs of his shoes had been taken out and placed in a neat row on the floor. I've since heard that the ghost of a maid haunts this room, tidying up the mess left by guests. Our experiences were weird, but I dismissed them, figuring they probably had a natural explanation. They reminded me of the stories surrounding the Stanley Hotel, whose guests report their personal possessions also being moved, and their clothes being mysteriously packed and unpacked.

Ironically, I now work at the Stanley Hotel where I am the resident illusionist. Every week I present theatrical séances that give guests a chance to experience what it would have been like to attend a spiritualist séance in the Victorian or Edwardian era. I use historical artifacts to transport the audience back in time, and I use the techniques of the fraudulent mediums to bring the spirits to life for 90 minutes of ghost stories and contrived paranormal encounters.

The Stanley Hotel
(Photo: Matthew Baxter)

I arrived at the Stanley Hotel as an illusionist and a skeptic. I have friends who have experienced strange events in their lives that made them believers in the paranormal, and I respect the fact that they truly believed their experiences were supernatural. But I myself regarded the idea of ghosts and hauntings as something intangible. Until I experience something really mysterious for myself, I resolved to keep an open mind, but I did not believe there was anything in this world that I could not explain.

That would all change in the Music Room.

My show is presented in various rooms on the hotel property. In the summer, the show is most often held in the Mac Gregor Ballroom, but once winter sets in we move to one of the smaller spaces that is equipped with a fireplace. During the winter season the show is usually presented in the Music Room.

This is a very special room in the hotel. It has been restored to the way it looked on opening day July 4, 1909, when it was a ladies writing room. It is thought to have been the favorite room of Mrs. Flora Stanley, the wife of F.O. Stanley, the hotel proprietor. On a small stage in this room there resides a Steinway piano. It was a gift to Flora from her devoted husband. Flora was said to have played that piano every day until she died.

It is believed that Flora haunts this room.

And it is here that I had a strange experience which has made me question my view of reality.

On April 7, 2016, I got married at the Stanley Hotel and we held our ceremony and reception in the Music Room. On a lark, my wife and I decided to do something quirky for our wedding. Since we met at the hotel during a show one night, we realized that if not for Flora and F.O. Stanley, we would not be getting married, so we set them a private table for the wedding reception. It was nothing grand. Just a table for two with a bunch of flowers and place settings laid in honor of the couple who built this amazing hotel and remained together for many years.

We didn't have time for a honeymoon because I had been scheduled to perform over the next few days. So, the day after our wedding I returned to the Music Room to do the shows for the weekend. It was during the third and final show that something strange occurred.

The show began as usual with some announcements about taking photos and silencing cell phones. Yet as these began, something odd occurred. The lights above the historic piano flickered on and off.

**The Music Room
(Photo: Aiden Sinclair)**

By this time, I had been performing in the Music Room for several months, and this had never happened before. I should probably also tell you that when it comes to my shows, I can be a bit OCD. I prepare the room precisely for each performance. The lights are always set in the exact same position with the dimmers adjusted. Though the hotel is over a century old, it has been fully restored and updated and the wiring that supports these lights is of a contemporary design. I had never experienced a problem with the lights nor should there ever be one.

But it was not just the flickering light that caught my attention.

A woman sitting in the front row wore a terrified expression on her face. She had turned to look at the flickering light, as had most of the audience, but whereas everyone else simply looked back at me, she continued to turn her head back and forth as she made eye contact with me and then stared in a very focused way at the piano on the other side of the room. She frowned and nodded in that direction as if to say, "Look! Do you see *that?*"

The woman's face turned a little pale and her hands shook. But, the show must go on, so I continued with my performance. As I did, the main overhead lights in the Music Room began to flicker too. It happened at random moments throughout the night. With each flicker, the woman in the front row grew more restless and again seemed to make eye contact with something near the piano.

When the show ended I immediately walked over to her and asked if she was okay. She was now weeping silently and still looking back at the piano. She asked if she could speak with me in private. We waited for the other guests to file out of the room. Once we were alone the following dialogue took place:

"Mr. Sinclair, I'm not crazy!" she said. "I don't believe in ghosts but I need to understand what just happened. Did you see the lights flicker?"

"Yes, I did." I replied. "Everyone did."

"Did *you* make that happen?" she asked.

"No," I said honestly. "I assure you that I did not and this has never happened before. If that is what has upset you I'm very sorry but I'm sure it was nothing paranormal," I explained.

"The lights didn't bother me," she said. "It was the *woman* that freaked me out. Did you see her too?"

"What woman?" I asked.

"The woman standing next to the piano during your entire show," she replied. "She wore a long dress and looked like she was from another era. She spoke to me. Every time those lights flickered I heard her voice in my head. She said, 'Tell him I like his show'."

This woman appeared to be honest and deeply troubled by what she had just experienced. Her emotions seemed genuine. I think she truly believed everything she was telling me. I was deeply moved that she had this experience. Of course, I like the idea that Flora approved of my performance, but I did not see what this audience member had seen. I could only calm her and assure her that if she had truly seen this woman standing beside the piano, then it was not by my doing.

Several months passed before I performed in the Music Room again, and this is when I had an experience that made me question things myself.

Several hours before the show I went to the local store to purchase some batteries needed for some small portable spotlights. As I was checking out I noticed a display of floral arrangements. They were fishbowl-like arrangements, each with a half dozen red roses in a glass bowl and a bow tied around the glass. I honestly don't know why, but I decided on the spot to buy a bunch of flowers for Flora.

I returned to the hotel and entered the Music Room, closing the door behind me. I was alone in the room and all of the lights were completely off. The shades were drawn and the room was lit by sunlight streaming in from an open patio door.

As I approached Flora's piano I was definitely thinking about the woman from the audience who had such a strange experience back in April. I set the roses on top of the piano and looked up at the lights above. Then, for some reason, I felt compelled to say something out loud to the empty room.

"Flora, if you are really here... thank you."

The lights blinked on and off twice.

Blink. Blink. Nothing more.

That should have been impossible. The lights were powered off. Yet it happened just the same, and to this very day I have no explanation for my mysterious experience in the Music Room.

Aiden Sinclair is America's preeminent grifter turned professional magician. After spending nearly two decades on the run from the law, he surrendered to federal agents and confessed to his life of confidence schemes and aliases. Five years in prison gave Aiden the opportunity to set out upon a new path in life. Rather than face a future as a recidivism statistic, he chose to spend his time adapting the skills that served him so well as a confidence artist to a new calling. Today, he practices the art of deception for your entertainment. Aiden has performed around the globe for thousands of spectators, including Hollywood celebrities and royalty, and he's been seen in living rooms across the nation on the hit NBC talent competition *America's Got Talent*. Aiden hosts the show *Illusions of the Passed* at the historic Stanley Hotel in Estes Park, Colorado. www.aidensinclair.net

The Ghosts Of Veteran's Park

Alison Smith

For me, the paranormal is a toy. I take it from its box when I have the desire to feel fear in a pure form. I feel it as an intense emotion; an essential piece of my humanity. Perhaps my disbelief in the supernatural makes it easier to pretend, but I sleep with lights burning; both dispelling the darkness and forming shadows in the corners that twist and lick with the passing of cars outside my window; giving the illusion of a hungry monster's movements. There's no such thing as ghosts. Of course. The world would be illogical with their inclusion—passing through walls, but not the floor; wearing period clothes and translucent luminescence; haunting dolls, but not Rubik's cubes.

"We should go to the woods," I say.

I suggest this to all my friends on nights when we are bored. It was a game of pretend for me—no different than playing with Barbie; except now I'm a teenager and games of imagination are more fun when no one sees it's a game.

Veteran's Park
(Photo: Arlington Parks & Recreation)

To convince them to come with me to Veteran's Park in Arlington, Texas, I relay a series of stories—none of which took place. Nothing significant ever happened there outside the annual botanical garden celebration and the sheer number of bunny rabbits that populate the fields during mating season. Oh, but the stories I tell...

An old man murdered his whole family in the abandoned house that backs on the park.

A little girl, abducted and murdered at the tree line, who peers out between the branches.

A teenage boy who fell from the rope swing: It still hangs from the tree. Catch it at the hour of his death, and his shadow swings again.

Deb wants to join me. She is my assistant manager at the fast food joint where I work. She envisions herself as Batman, a firefighter, and an astronaut rolled into one woman who fears nothing, and will conquer even the shadows.

"Is that safe?" Brad asks.

We stand in the back room after closing time. I slice tomatoes for the next day's lunch rush, taking care not to slice a finger off like they advise you in the safety video. Brad leans against the metal preparation table. He clears his throat, looks down, and places his palm against the table as if reading its vibrations; perhaps remembering last week, when he stood in the exact same spot and cried after a customer yelled at him when he made a mistake with her order.

Deb stifles a laugh, dunks the last dish into the bleach water, and turns to us.

"I swear to protect you," she says with a salute.

Craig leans out of the walk-in refrigerator, puffing on a joint, the inventory clipboard he was supposed to fill out lost somewhere inside.

"Yeah, pussy," he says to Brad. "We won't let anything get you."

I stop cutting the tomatoes, step back, and face them all.

"We'll be fine," I say. "As long as you don't make them... *angry*."

We take Deb's car, The Batmobile, to the park. Deb and Craig sit in the front seats, laughing about the ghosts and what they'll look like. What they'll do if one comes for us. Deb will rush toward it. Craig will throw a rock at its head. He looks over his shoulder at Brad, whose hands are twisted in his lap like a knotted charm.

"Brad, you can just piss yourself," Craig says. "No self-respecting ghost would go near your stink."

Craig waits for Brad to respond, but nothing comes, so he flips on the radio. We park outside the apartment complex across the street, knowing that the park is closed for the night. We start the trek to the entrance, but Deb pauses.

"Wait!" she cries, and runs back to her car. She opens the trunk and pulls out a mini tape recorder, waving it proudly. "In case the ghosts talk," she says, as she hits the record button.

Near the front of the park there is a playground, and the swings rock gently in the breeze. A concrete path runs a mile around the fields, with an amphitheater and a duck pond tucked inside. The streetlamps are so bright, yet they are unable to dispel the eerie quietness of the place. The tree line past the concrete path beckons, the limbs waving to the heavens; or to us. I was never sure.

Even Craig falls silent as we head towards the trees. The line seems impenetrable unless you have experience behind you, and I pull aside a branch, revealing a dark, narrow path that leads to a stream with a two-by-four plank laid across it to act as a bridge.

Deb goes first; then me; then Brad; then Craig. We emerge onto a plain of sandstone.

The layout of Veteran's Park is confusing, and my mind has never grasped the design of the trails. You think you know which way you're headed, but then wind up back at its beginning, unsure of what happened. Certain landmarks stand in the place—The Trapped Trail; where the trail dips and the sides rise and you stand enclosed between six foot high walls of dirt, unable to see beyond it because the branches of the lining trees stretch all the way across the sky to block out even the moonlight. There is a pavilion at the top of a hill with benches and a footbridge leading to the botanic garden. Everything else is grey and directionless in the darkness.

"Which way do we go?" Deb asks.

Veteran's Park
(Photo: Alison Smith)

I take the lead and turn right, headed for the first landmark I know—The Trapped Trail. The scariest part is that there is nowhere to run but forward or back, and if something comes for you, you're done for. I walk fast and sure; past a pile of rocks I know; our feet sinking in a puddle of muck. I turn right again, and know that we are on the trail. The rising of the walls is a slow process. It is hard to notice at first, until the danger of being trapped lands in your consciousness and the claustrophobia sets in. The narrowness of the trail forces us into single file. Deb brings up the rear now with Brad walking behind me, so close that his quickened breath is on my neck. Craig walks just behind Brad.

A snapping sound echoes from the trees on the right; followed by another to the left. I stop suddenly, and Brad slams into me.

"Sorry," he says.

"Are there animals here?" Deb asks from the back of the line.

Then there is another sharp snapping sound from the left again. And an answer from the right. I pull my phone from my pocket and shine the light on the others.

"Craig, you dick," I say. One of his hands is full of rocks while the other covers his mouth to keep him from laughing out loud.

"You… should've… seen his face," he says.

As I roll my eyes, a rustle sounds from the branches above us. I swing my phone's light upwards, and the limbs crack aside as a massive shadow swoops down. Deb yells at us to run, and it's chaos.

Craig tries to push past her while Brad tries to push past him. I scan the trees trying to see what the shadow could've been. Something gives, and Craig is gone, far ahead with Brad just behind him. Deb and I run too, trying to keep up.

"Faster!" Deb cries, and I'm not sure if she's talking to herself or me.

We reach the end of the Trapped Trail, and find Brad on his back, clutching his ankle. Craig stands ten feet off, too afraid to walk back toward us and whatever monster was in the trees. Deb's hero instincts take over, and she holds Brad down while she checks his wound.

"It's just a bruise," she tells him, "Just a bruise. Let's go." She gives him a hand up.

"What the fuck was that?" Craig yells.

Brad leans against Deb and gestures back to the Trapped Trail. "What the hell do you think?" he says. "It was a ghost!"

My heart beats fast, but it's funny. Because ghosts don't exist. Of course.

I point to the top of the hill.

"There's a pavilion up there with benches," I say, "I know the way out from there."

We walk up the hill in silence, a streetlamp at the top guiding us; the world too quiet to feel safe. The minutes it takes drag like hours; Craig turning on the light from his phone every few seconds to shoot it at the plain around us in case we've garnered the interest of Something. The path we take twists behind the pavilion. In a small clearing, someone has arranged hundreds of rocks into the shape of a heart. It feels menacing instead of sweet. We stumble around the building, and fall into seats at the bench, safe in the light.

On this side, giant bushes run against the edge of the decline of the hill. Their leaves wave at us while we sit in silence, gathering ourselves. We can see the parking lot from here, far in the distance, but along the bright concrete path that means safety.

"I don't know what the fuck that was," Craig says, "but I'm glad we're leaving."

A thunk sounds from the hillside. And another. And another. We hear footsteps; but they sound bigger than a human's. Louder; closer; one after the other—thunk. Thunk. Thunk.

"Craig, what the fuck are you doing?" Brad asks.

But Craig holds his hands up to show they're empty; a kind of choking sound escaping him.

I look at the others and they all have the same openmouthed expression; frozen; unsure what to do. Thunk. Thunk. Right upon us now. We draw a collective breath. The entire line of giant bushes shakes as though something massive standing behind them has grabbed hold and is pulling them in a fury. Craig screams again, breaking the frozenness that settled upon us, and we run; run for the light; for the car. I throw looks over my shoulder as I go, trying to see if anything emerges; but the shaking stops and nothing reveals itself. We fly to the footbridge where we pause again, gasping for breath.

"Why the fuck did you bring us here, Alison?" Brad asks, and I'm not really sure anymore.

The paranormal is just something you take out of the box and play with. But I smile.

"It was probably animals," I say, "No big deal."

I walk to the end of the footbridge and onto the safety of the concrete path. At this point, the path reaches a crossroads. Going left will take you back toward the woods; going straight leads to the car, to the right is the street. I turn left and take a couple of steps.

"Come on. Let's go just a little furth..."

I was interrupted by screaming. It sounded like a woman, but it couldn't have been. Whatever it was it didn't stop to breathe. Just scream after scream; overlapping impossibly.

They ran; all yelling unintelligible things, leaving me standing there, trying to figure out the sound, trying to figure out how it could exist. I snapped back to reality.

"Don't you want to find out where it's coming from?" I yelled after them.

But no answer came; just their yells on the wind. I gave up, and followed.

We ran all the way to the car. We could still hear the screams from there. The exact same pattern; that impossible overlap. We threw ourselves into the car, and peeled out of the parking lot. Driving too fast and too scared. Thinking a million things simultaneously.

"Deb," I say, "Let me see the tape recorder."

She tosses it to me, and I know the part I want to hear. I rewind to the moment the screaming started; listening again, searching for the answer. We all hear it at the same time. On the recording, outside of the screaming, you can hear us all yelling.

I am far off, and yelling "Don't you want to find out where it's coming from?"

Deb is yelling "Keep going, keep going."

Craig is yelling "What the fuck?"

Brad is yelling, "We're going to fucking die!"

But we could also hear what sounded like laughter.

"Turn it off," Deb orders.

I do, and hand the recorder back. We continue our ride in silence.

In recalling this story, I grew curious about the park. As I said, nothing of note ever happened there, so even if all of this was unexplainable, surely it wasn't ghosts. So I searched again. This time I found some new information.

In 1985, a couple was stabbed to death in Veteran's Park. Their murders were never solved.

But, of course, there's no such thing as ghosts.

Of course.

Alison Smith is a writer and the former Program Manager for the James Randi Educational Company for over three years, where she oversaw the Million Dollar Paranormal Challenge and created marketing and promotional campaigns for the organization.

Throwing Some Light On The Subject

Blake Smith

In October of 1997 my friend Ted and I were taking a paranormal-themed road trip across the United States.

We left Gulf Breeze, Florida, where we'd just visited a UFO hotspot, and headed north to Interstate 10. The weather was clear and cooling down, and we had to cross a lot of territory to get to Louisiana. According to our map it was about 200 miles to New Orleans, and that would take around 3 hours. The Samurai wouldn't do much above 65 mph—at that point she was literally maxed out. Pedal touching floor, that's all she'd do.

"Can't this thing hit 70?" Ted asked.

"Yeah, but we'd have to drive it off a cliff. Maybe if we make a stop at the Grand Canyon?"

"That's pathetic," he said.

I'm not sure if he meant my joke or the Samurai. I bought her used, but she's already a ten-year-old car and has seen the better part of her service. Still, she's cranked every time I've tried so far this trip. That's good enough for me.

"You know anything about ghosts or voodoo?" asked Ted.

"Not much about voodoo, but I've done a lot of background research on ghosts," I replied.

"Do you believe in them?"

"I don't know. I've seen some weird stuff, but not a ghost exactly. But if you could prove ghosts exist, then you'd prove there was life after death, right? And that gets right to the heart of the paranormal. We want proof that there is something beyond the mundane. Everybody would like to know that."

"Yeah—that's true," he said. "What kind of weird things are you talking about?"

"Well, we've got some time to kill so I'll tell you about the weird stuff that happened to me while I was in the navy."

"On a ship?"

"No. It was while I was stationed in Bahrain in 1992-93."

We're crossing lonely stretches of Interstate 10, much of it alternating between woodland and black-water swamp. I'm back to worrying about crashing off a bridge into the water, but the storytelling distracts me.

"When I arrived in Bahrain they put me in a hotel until I could find an apartment to rent."

"You didn't have to stay on the base?" Ted asked. "I thought you said you slept on base."

"Well, when we were on duty we stayed on base overnight, but usually we ended up sleeping in our apartments. I found a place to rent that was very close to base in a nice, modern high-rise. And for the first few months, except for some problems with the elevator occasionally getting stuck, it was peaceful. There was a movie rental place around the corner that had mostly pirated stuff for just a dinar. And the best shawarma was right down the street. That's like a gyro only better. The chicken shawarma was served up with chopped cabbage and hot sauce. It was delicious."

The Apartment In Bahrain
(Photo: Blake Smith)

"Boy, you sure know how to tell a scary story," Ted said with a fake yawn.

"Anyway, one night I'm doing my usual off-duty routine, renting a couple of movies and having some shawarma. I get through my movies, which I must admit were mostly 1960s Amicus and Hammer horror flicks, and then head to bed. I hadn't been in bed very long when suddenly I felt something pounce onto me. It felt like a person had just sat on my chest. I freak out, struggle with this thing and then finally manage to jump out of bed. I hit the light and expected a fight. I was ready to rumble!"

Ted laughed.

"I look at the bed and there's a lump in the middle like a person is laying under the covers. So I attack it! But the bulge collapses. I pull the cover off the bed. Nothing. I look under the bed. Nobody. I check the closet and the bathroom. The bedroom door is locked, and the door was never opened. There is a window, but it's closed. I think about it for a minute. I'm a trained security policeman, so I call into the TOC—"

"The what?"

"The Tactical Operations Center. They're the dispatch desk for the base security force. I told the petty officer that I've had an intruder. He knows me and asks if I'm ok. I tell him I'm fine and then explain what happened. He says there is no fucking way he is going to write up that I was assaulted by a ghost and put it in the logbook with his name beside it. He tells me to stop wasting his time and go back to bed. If anybody that I can actually see shows up I should kick their ass, subdue them and then call back."

Ted laughed again.

"Yeah, it was funny later on. At the time, it pissed me off. I was scared. My heart was racing and I didn't want to turn off the light. Which is silly when you think about it. I mean, my day job was to ride around in a boat with a machine-gun on the front, looking for terrorists. When I wasn't doing that I was patrolling the base bar looking to bust up fights with Marines. None of *that* scared me at all, but invisible assailants *did*. So I went back to bed, but I left the light on. For many nights to come, I left the lights on."

"Did it ever happen again?"

"I'm getting to that. Don't rush me." I said. "The next thing that happened was that I started having electrical problems. Two televisions went out and because I was staying in a furnished apartment they had to replace them. Then the light bulbs started exploding."

"Exploding?"

"Well, there wasn't a fire or anything, but before this if a bulb went out it would flare-up and then go out. Or it would just go out. Suddenly my bulbs started going out with alarming regularity, and when they did the glass shattered all over the place. Then I'd have to cut the power and use a pair of pliers to get the bulb stem out of the socket."

"That's weird," Ted said. "Did you change brands of bulbs?"

"I tried many different brands and different wattages but sooner or later they all exploded and shot glass everywhere. Then two electric hot-water heaters exploded, spraying steaming hot water all over my bathrooms. The landlord was getting mad at me for all the repairs. No one else in the building was having similar problems.

"Then, my great-uncle Jack, who was like a grandfather to me, suffered a stroke and I had to fly home because we thought he was going to die. Thankfully he didn't, but when I was returning from leave I had to wait a week to get a flight back to Bahrain so I was stuck on a layover in Philadelphia. And while I was at the airport motel, my invisible intruder returned. This time I knew I was alone because the door was chained and bolted. I got out of bed, went to see the night manager and asked if anybody had died in the room I was staying in.

"He acted like I was an axe-murderer and told me to go back to my room or he would call the police. He wouldn't even let me into the office but left me standing out in the cold. So I went back to the room and called a friend of mine who was working a late shift in Atlanta and I told him I was freaking out about this invisible assailant. He listened and was very rational about the whole issue. After a while I felt better and went back to sleep—with the lights on.

"Finally, back in Bahrain, when it was getting close to the holidays, I threw a Christmas party. I invited my friend Tom, who worked with me at the Harbor Patrol, and he invited some British ex-patriots who lived in his building. They were all really nice and it was a good little party with lots of Brits walking around swilling wine and talking about how they missed England during Christmas time. Tom told me that the wife of one of the guests was coming straight to the party from the airport. I'd never met the man or his wife, and at ten o'clock that night she rang the doorbell and I opened the door. Did you ever see the movie *Don't Look Now*?" I asked.

"Yeah," Ted replied.

"Remember those two British psychics?"

He nodded.

"Well, this lady looked like one of them. She doesn't say 'Merry Christmas' or 'Thanks for letting me come with no notice,' —instead she just walks in, looks around and says, 'There is a presence here.'

She goes on to tell me that she can sense it is a feminine spirit that seeks to comfort me, and means me no harm. Then, once I'm completely freaked out, she spots her husband in the room and walks off into the party."

"That's weird," Ted said.

"You're telling me. Well, I didn't change my behavior because of it—I just kept sleeping with the lights on. But I decided I'd get a dog because I'd read that they can see ghosts. So I got myself a dog and named him Mr. Pooky."

"I remember Mr. Pooky," said Ted.

"I got him when he was about three months old. He loved that apartment. And… the light bulbs stopped exploding! But he would sit in the living room and growl at the windows. We were five stories up, and there was a little terrace that looked out over Bahrain. He barked and growled at that window unless I closed the door and the curtains. But as long as Mr. Pooky was there, the activity stopped.

"Flash forward a few years later. I was out of the navy at back in the states. Mr. Pooky and I moved into the house where my uncle Jack used to live. After I was there about a year, Mr. Pooky was hit by a truck and I had to put him down. Not much after that, guess what started happening?"

"I don't know," said Ted.

"The light bulbs started exploding again! This freaked me out even worse than before. A friend of mine from Tennessee was staying with me. You may remember Curtis?"

Ted nodded.

"Well, he thought the house needed a spiritual cleansing. I told him if he wanted to get a priest or something to go ahead—but as a protestant, I didn't think it would help. In fact, I ended up calling a priest and asking about it and was told that he would bless my house, but that he didn't generally do exorcisms or spiritual cleansings. Besides, was it even the house that was the problem? In Bahrain, Philadelphia and Cartersville—the common factor was *me*, not the place. But Curtis lit a smudge stick and walked around the house saying prayers. After that, no more light bulbs exploded."

"So you think he cleansed the house of evil?" asked Ted.

"I don't know."

"Why's that? It sounds like it was effective."

"I can't say. I think it is because when it comes down to it, the activity that most disturbed me was something crawling into my bed. After I got out of the navy I did some research and discovered a phenomenon called sleep paralysis. Roughly speaking, this is when you're half asleep, but paralyzed, and having free-form dreams mixed with reality. One of the most common effects is the feeling that someone or something is sitting on your chest. It is likely the cause for the belief in succubus and incubus demons. And it has a remarkable resemblance to alien abduction cases in which people say they've felt alien intelligence was watching them. Whether they thought their experience was caused by demons, angels, or aliens depended on the person and their beliefs."

"Where'd you hear about this?" Ted asked.

"There is a lot on sleep paralysis in books about the paranormal. The trouble with these is that the skeptical books usually debunk everything without allowing for the possibility of the paranormal while the believer's books are often completely credulous."

We drive on. The suspension on the Samurai is terrible and the road switches from blacktop to concrete slabs. Every few feet we hit a bump, which drives up the frame of the car and slams into my lower back. I'm pretty sure I'm going to be an inch shorter or in need of a wheelchair by the time we reach New Orleans.

"So you never did see a ghost?" asked Ted.

"No, but I cleaned up a shitload of broken light bulbs."

Blake Smith is a writer, researcher and IT professional. He's also the producer and a host of the podcast Monster Talk, the science show about monsters. He lives with his wife and children in Georgia, along with a pair of emotionally distant cats.

The Poltergeist In The Bakery

Hayley Stevens

If the stories are true, The Shires Shopping Centre in Trowbridge, England, is haunted.

The site on which it stands has a long and rich history. It was an Iron Age hill fort used by the Celts as they defended the area against the invading Romans. During the Middle Ages, Trowbridge Castle stood on the grounds. From the 14th century, the town developed as a center for the production of woolen cloth. And in more recent times, the Shires Shopping Centre opened in 1990.

The Shires Shopping Centre
(Photo: Wikipedia)

I grew up in and around Trowbridge. When I finished school I found a job in a bakery in The Shires Shopping Centre where I worked for almost three years. This shop was the setting for some of the weirdest things that I have ever witnessed and these experiences prompted me to become an investigator of mysterious phenomena. I've now been researching the topic of ghosts for over a decade after having a life-long interest in the subject. I don't believe in ghosts, but I have had experiences that I can't explain. I present my story not as evidence of anything in particular, but because I think skeptics do a disservice to those we try to help if we don't talk about the peculiar things that *we ourselves* have experienced.

I hadn't heard about the ghost stories in the bakery until the first time somebody (or something) untied my apron. I'd been working in the back section of the bakery, preparing fresh sandwiches for the day when my apron spun around my body so that it was only hanging around my neck. This surprised me because I had tied the apron strings firmly at the back with a double knot!

I turned to the woman working with me and said, "My apron just *undid* itself!"

"Ah, you've met Joshua!" she replied.

The staff believed a little boy named Joshua haunted the shop. Some thought he had died in the woolen mills during the 1500s. Others said he was a peasant boy from the time the castle stood.

I wasn't sure what to make of my experience because aprons can undo themselves and knots work loose, right? It was likely a coincidence, but it kept happening. On occasion, everyone working there would find their aprons untied simultaneously.

But there was also the voice. When we worked at the sandwich bar we'd be out of view of the public. Our backs faced the exit at the rear of the store that opened up into a dark passageway leading outside. There were occasions when we'd be working in this area and we'd hear our names called out in an eerie singsong voice.

"That's Joshua," one of my older colleagues always insisted as I checked to see if anyone was hiding out of sight. I never did find anyone.

I didn't considered these incidents to be proof of the paranormal. They could have just been coincidences, or maybe somebody messing around and tricking us. When your mind is focused on baguettes and sausage rolls you're not always aware of your surroundings. It would be easy for a practical joker to throw his or her voice and run away, or to give your apron string a sneaky pull when you're distracted, and then blame "Joshua."

Yet, during my time working in the shop there were two specific incidents that truly spooked me.

The first happened one morning shortly after we opened the shop. I was serving customers at the front counter. We had four large display cabinets next to one another that we worked behind. At each end of these cabinets was a fastened metal security gate, designed to restrict the public from getting behind the counters. I was serving the only customers in the store, a couple who bought a loaf of sliced bread. The loaves of bread sat on a shelf about five feet off of the floor at the opposite end of the counter to where I stood. As I turned to make my way to the bread display the security gate at the other end of the counter flew open on its own. It burst open with such a force that several loaves of bread toppled off the shelf and fell to the floor.

The customers gasped. The clamor caused one of my colleagues to rush out to the front of the shop to see what had happened. He was concerned that someone had forced their way behind the counter.

"You've obviously got a ghost in here!" said the lady I was serving.

My colleague and I exchanged an alarmed look.

Once the customers had gone we tried to recreate the gate swinging open but it just wouldn't budge unless it was lifted up first.

The second incident took a more violent turn.

On occasion I worked a shift with a girl with whom I had gone to school. It's fair to say that she and I were not friends but we attempted to be polite and courteous to one another at work. On this particular morning I felt she wasn't pulling her weight although it was one of the busiest days of the week. I grew angrier and angrier that the rest of us had to do more work to make up for her laziness. The manager asked her to clean up the sandwich bar after they finished the sandwich preparation. As she did this reluctantly I muttered something akin to, "Finally doing some work..." This generated the kind of atmosphere that only two teenage girls who are furious with one another can create.

I was in charge of the hot food section. Next to the ovens where I was working was the cleaning area where she was working. Between both of us stood a tall free standing shelving unit where we placed kitchenware to dry. She filled up the dishwasher and when the items were clean she emptied the contents into this unit (between checking her mobile phone and avoiding work by hiding out in the staff room.) I could see her doing this because we were working in such close quarters. It made me very cross, so I decided that the next time she emerged from the staff room I was going to speak my mind. But when she returned to empty the dishwasher I didn't get my chance to say anything at all. We were standing just a few feet away from one another when the entire contents of the drying unit came crashing down around us. Big metal tubs, silverware, spatulas, large (and very sharp) knives, metal strainers and baking sheets flew off the shelves. The objects seemed to *explode* out of the shelving unit, hitting the wall and fridges behind us as we both cringed and cowered. Strangely, nothing hit us.

From my position in the store I was able to see everyone who was at work that day and there was no one else there with us. My old school mate and I were the only ones in the rear of the store, and the back exit was locked.

Colleagues in the front of the shop came running to see what had happened. It was like something out of the movie *Ghostbusters*, only instead of getting covered with slime, *we* got covered with utensils. At least they were clean, I suppose.

This particular incident has stayed fresh in my mind because I still have no idea how it happened. I've been able to look back at other experiences and eventually figure out the cause. But not with this one. I have been investigating anomalous phenomena for over a decade now and in that time I have not witnessed anything of that nature again.

It wasn't long after this that I started to watch the TV show "Most Haunted" (and yes, I believed it all to be true at the time). I studied the work of well-known British paranormal researchers Peter Underwood, Harry Price, Guy Lyon Playfair, and many others. I learned that *they* would consider this to be poltergeist activity triggered by teenage hormones. Objects thrown at people only to avoid making contact and not causing harm are said to be common in these cases. This was a prominent feature in the 1966 Black Monk of Pontefract case, as well as the Enfield poltergeist case of the 1970s.

Soon after my interest in ghosts began to grow, "Most Haunted" found itself in the middle of a scandal. Until that point I had trusted the show as my number one resource for paranormal information. It connected the viewer to what I perceived to be the modern world of ghost research. I trusted it even more than the books I borrowed from the library! Disillusioned, I decided to form my own paranormal investigation team. I was 18 when I started to lead a small group of other ghost enthusiasts into local businesses that were believed to be haunted.

A year later that I met another local ghost hunter named Ray Jorden. Ray is now a star on the TV show "Haunting Australia," but at the time we were both new to the scene. I joined Ray on a few ghost hunts across the county of Wiltshire. One day he asked if I'd like to join him and some others for an investigation at a local shopping centre. Then I discovered the investigation was to be held at The Shires Shopping Centre. This could be my chance to discover what was going on. What had rained knives down on me? What had slammed that security gate open? Were we dealing with a poltergeist? Was the shop haunted? Was Joshua real?

"Yes!" I replied.

The night arrived and we all met outside the shopping centre just as it started to grow dark. We didn't have access to the shops but we didn't need that because ghosts can walk through walls, right? I was a little frightened when I realized that the others had decided to make their base right outside the bakery where I had worked. With the shops closed for the evening and the customers gone, the place took on a more ominous feel. We hadn't even started the investigation before strange things began to happen. We were talking among ourselves when it became clear that someone was humming. But that someone wasn't us. When we hushed each other the humming stopped suddenly. Then someone laughed.

It sounded like a child.

Throughout the evening people reported hearing someone whistling at them. One lady even claimed that someone kept tugging on her shirt.

Since then I have popped into the bakery on many occasions to buy food. The last time I visited, none of the original team was working there anymore and the security gates had gone. As I stood in line I wondered if this time I'd have the courage to ask the staff if they have ever experienced weird things in the store. But I didn't. It would be wrong of me to suggest that the shop has a resident ghost. This could bring distress to the current employees, and I don't want to be *that* customer. Besides, although weird incidents happened to me this doesn't mean the place is haunted. Just because I don't have an explanation doesn't mean there isn't one. We humans are pattern-seeking creatures, right? What's to say that I didn't link these individual occurrences when they're not connected at all? When I worked in the shop we didn't have a skeptical paranormal researcher around to solve the mystery for us. The legends grew each time something slightly unusual happened, and we reinforced the belief that something paranormal was happening.

"That's Joshua," we'd say.

"Thanks a lot, Joshua."

"Go away, Joshua."

"Oh bloody hell, Joshua!"

Nowadays, when I conduct investigations I try to work out what information is missing from the claims. These details help to build the bigger picture and pinpoint the causes of alleged paranormal phenomena.

I just hope that the woman I went to school with doesn't believe I'm the cause of the strange events that took place at the bakery, like I'm some sort of real-life Carrie out of a Stephen King novel. But thinking about it, she never did annoy me again after that.

Hayley Stevens is a paranormal researcher who doesn't believe in the paranormal but instead attempts to find rational causes for the weird things people claim to experience. She lives in Wiltshire, England, and investigates reports of paranormal activity using scientific skepticism. Hayley has lectured across Europe about her rational approaches to paranormal investigation. She is often sought by the media for her opinions and thoughts on strange stories. http://hayleyisaghost.co.uk

The Rose Of Tralee

Karen Stollznow

My grandmother used to live in Katoomba, a popular holiday destination west of Sydney, Australia. The town is famous for its backdrop of the Blue Mountains, a national park with breathtaking views that is home to a unique sandstone formation called the Three Sisters. The Blue Mountains are so-named because dense forests of eucalyptus trees release oils into the air that create a blue haze across the sky. The place has a magical quality to it; with its mountain scenery, its caves full of Aboriginal rock art, its rare native plants and animals, and rumors that the gorges and forests are home to a strange beast known as the Yowie.

**The Three Sisters
(Photo: Matthew Baxter)**

When I was a young girl I'd catch the train from Sydney to Katoomba during the school holidays to visit my grandmother. This was a two-hour journey so I'd usually pass the time reading books about ghosts. My grandmother would meet me at the train station and from there we'd go out for ice cream. Clutching her ice cream cone in one hand, she chatted so excitedly that it melted and dripped down her arm.

We spent our time together searching for knick-knacks in antique stores, planting peppermint in her garden, and making bread and butter pudding for dessert. During one of these visits she noticed my ghost books and said mysteriously, "I have a story to tell you."

One Monday morning, she was shopping in her local K-Mart. The store was busy and pop music played loudly. All of a sudden, the music ground to a halt and the store went silent. The bright fluorescent lights went dim, and there were no other customers in sight. She was completely alone when, out of nowhere, a ghostly female voice started singing.

The pale moon was rising above the green mountain,
The sun was declining beneath the blue sea,
When I strayed with my love to the pure crystal fountain,
That stands in the beautiful vale of Tralee.

She recognized the tune immediately. It was the Irish folk song *The Rose of Tralee*. Her parents were Irish immigrants and her father, Tom, used to sing the song to her when she was a little girl. It was his favorite song. As the eerie music played she thought of him and at that very moment he appeared in front of her.

She couldn't believe her eyes. This was *impossible*. He had been buried the week before.

Yet there he was, standing right in front of her. She thought he looked handsome and younger.

"Don't worry, Ruby," he said. "I'm fine."

Then he vanished.

The lights brightened in the store again and the pop music resumed. The customers reappeared and continued shopping as though nothing had happened. Everything was back to normal although my grandmother was in shock. She believed she had seen her father's ghost. This was his chance to see her one last time and reassure her that he was okay.

My grandmother was a sensible, no-nonsense woman who was not prone to fantasy or telling stories. Had it been me who had reported a visit from my great-grandfather's ghost, I would have gotten into trouble for telling tall tales! But my grandmother swore that this incident happened, and for the rest of her life told the story many times.

The Former K-Mart Building
(Photo: Blue Mountains Gazette)

How can I explain my grandmother's ghostly encounter? First of all, it's difficult to explain someone else's personal experience. Without being there myself, and not being able to recreate the event, I can't ever know for sure what happened. All I can do is suggest a possible explanation.

After a loved one dies, many people see ghosts. In his *Scientific American* article "Ghost Stories: Visits from the Deceased," psychiatrist Vaughan Bell says that our deceased loved ones, "remain in our hearts and minds, of course, but for many people they also linger in our senses—as sights, sounds, smells, touches or presences."

These reactions to bereavement are known as grief hallucinations or illusions.

It is surprisingly common for grieving people to experience hallucinations of their deceased loved ones, including their pets. Various studies show that a staggering 50% of people have these experiences after someone has died. In fact, grief hallucinations are so common that they are considered a normal reaction to loss. They are found across cultures and beliefs, and play an important part in the grieving and healing process as they help those who are in mourning to cope and adjust to the change, and even maintain a bond with their lost loved one. Some people find the experience unsettling or even frightening, although many find it provides comfort and solace, especially when it is seen in a spiritual or religious context. For many, these experiences are proof that there is life after death and that we will be reunited with our friends and families one day.

Usually, people who have a grief hallucination keep it to themselves. They are reluctant to share the experience because they feel embarrassed and fear that no one will believe them. They even wonder if they're going insane. However, experiencing a grief hallucination doesn't mean that the person suffers from a mental illness, or that they were drunk or on drugs at the time. We are so attuned to the presence of our loved ones that, when they are no longer there, we still expect to see and hear them. The sense of loss is so great that we are watchful for signs of them and our minds unconsciously fill in the gaps. We are not ready to let go. As renowned neurologist Oliver Sacks says in his book *Hallucinations*, "Losing a parent, a spouse, or a child is losing a part of oneself and bereavement causes a sudden hole in one's life, a hole which—somehow—must be filled."

Grief hallucinations occur most frequently around the time of death, but in some cases, they may continue for years afterwards. Sometimes they happen many years later. My friend Joe Anderson experienced a grief hallucination more than 20 years after his father's passing:

"I was in the bathroom at the time. I had just showered, shaved and put on a dress shirt. I pulled up the collar and started putting on my necktie when I had this… sensation. It was the absolutely real feeling of my father standing behind me. When I was a kid he taught me how to put on a tie. We would stand in front of the mirror together and he would place his big arms around me as he helped me to tie it. What happened that day was more than just a memory. It was an experience. I could feel his presence in the room. It was exactly like he was there with me. I felt him standing behind me, just like he did when I was a kid. I couldn't see him but the feeling was so strong that I even looked in the mirror to see if he was there. The strangest thing was that I could also smell his aftershave. It was like my father's ghost was right there with me; an invisible ghost of him that I could smell, feel, and sense."

Grief hallucinations can seem very real. People who experience them report intimate encounters, such as hearing the sound of their loved one's voice or smelling their perfume, just as Joe smelled his father's aftershave. Many people feel their loved ones give them a hug or a kiss, while in a large number of cases, the widowed feel their spouse climb into bed with them. People sense the presence of their loved one, even though they are no longer there. In some ways, grief hallucinations are similar to "phantom limb syndrome," a puzzling disorder in which people who've had a limb amputated have the vivid perception that it is still attached to their body and performing its normal functions.

Sometimes the living are visited by the dead in their dreams bringing positive and reassuring messages. Some catch a glimpse of the deceased out of the corner of their eye. Others see full apparitions that walk up the stairs or sit in their favorite chair. The deceased may have motives for their return, like my great grandfather appearing to his daughter to say, "Don't worry, Ruby. I'm fine." In some stories, they pay a visit to deal with unfinished business. In Shakespeare's *Hamlet*, the ghost of the prince's father showed up to reveal he was poisoned by his own brother, and to summon his son to avenge his death.

Grief hallucinations can also be triggered during reminders of the deceased. Being in the house where the person once lived or hearing a nostalgic song on the radio can prompt an experience. They can happen while performing a ritual or routine that is associated with the deceased, such as Joe tying his tie. In this way, these experiences are similar to a memory that transports people back to their past. As Joe put it, his experience was "...a memory that powerfully reinserted itself into my present. It was like a simultaneous playback and an experience at the same time."

Whether the experiencer believes in a natural or supernatural explanation, grief hallucinations can have a powerful, lasting effect and hold great personal significance.

Occasionally, people experience a grief hallucination *before* they know the person has died. Rather than being a psychic premonition or ghostly visitation, these experiences may be prompted by the knowledge that a loved one is sick or elderly and perhaps near death. In his afterword, Dr. James Alcock talks about this phenomenon.

A grief hallucination is just one possible explanation for what happened to my grandmother.

The night that she died I remembered her ghost story. I was home alone during a thunderstorm. I had a window open slightly and I could hear the storm raging outside. It was the perfect night for a haunting. I wondered if my grandmother might appear to me the way her father had appeared to her, all those years ago. I didn't believe in ghosts but the thought still made me a little nervous. The wind howled and the curtains moved as though there was someone standing behind them.

After a massive thunderbolt of lighting struck, my phone rang. I nearly jumped out of my skin. As I picked up the phone my hand shook a little.

"Hello?"

"Hello, dear," said my grandmother's voice as the line cracked and buzzed.

"But, Nana…you're dead," I replied in shock.

I heard a "click" and there was silence.

What had just happened?

Had my deceased grandmother called from beyond the grave to say, "Don't worry. I'm fine"?

I couldn't call the number back, these were the days before Caller ID, and so I waited for her to call again. But she never did.

Soon afterwards, my housemate arrived home and I told him about the spooky call. He was practical about the whole incident.

"Do you think it was just a wrong number?" he suggested. "Then the woman freaked out when you said, 'You're dead'. That would be a creepy thing to hear."

This made sense. At first I thought I'd heard my grandmother's voice but maybe I was mistaken. It was probably a stranger who had dialed the wrong number at the right time. Perhaps I had experienced an auditory grief hallucination. A coincidence was more likely than a phone call from a ghost, right?

I'll never know exactly what happened in either case. But it seems as though our brains generated these experiences because my grandmother wanted to see her father one last time, as I did her.

After all, no one can fool us like our own minds, especially when we want to believe.

Dr. Karen Stollznow is the author of the novel *Hits & Mrs.*, and the non-fiction books *God Bless America; Language Myths, Mysteries and Magic*, and *Haunting America*. A host of the Monster Talk podcast, she has spent many years investigating psychics, ghosts, Bigfoot and other paranormal claims. Also a linguist, she has taught at several universities in the United States and Australia, and she was a researcher at the University of California, Berkeley. Karen was born in Sydney, Australia, and she currently lives in Denver, Colorado. www.karenstollznow.com

Pulling My Leg

James Underdown

We are in a love affair with our own version of reality. We think that what we see, everyone sees, and what we hear, everyone hears. But I'm here to tell you to not completely trust your senses or the brains that organize them. None of us can be trusted to get it right all the time.

Years ago, when I was visiting my parents in suburban Chicago, I had a strange experience. It was late at night and I was in bed, dozing off, when I distinctly felt a hand firmly grab one of my calves. With my heart beating rapidly, I leapt out of bed and turned on all the lights. What the hell? But there was no one else in the room, and the door and windows were locked from the inside. Hercule Poirot would have had a tough time with this one…

My Parent's House
(Photo: James Underdown)

I should have prefaced my story by saying that my family has a long and storied history of capers and practical jokes, and that fact entered my mind in the initial moments of this drama. I quickly searched the area—looking under both single beds and in the closet—and double-checked the doors and windows. The space was devoid of pranksters. Indeed, none of the usual suspects were even in town!

That left three possibilities.

1. The usual suspects had constructed an ingenious gimmick to grab my calf in such a way that their machinations would disappear without a trace through locked doors and windows.

2. A ghost or some kind of spirit took it upon itself to drop into *that* room *that* night and mess with me for no apparent reason.

3. I dreamt it.

Occam's Razor—the line of reasoning that we should favor the simplest hypothesis with the fewest assumptions—helped me to eliminate numbers 1 and 2 pretty quickly. (At this point, solving the mystery was more important to me than being alarmed.) No one I knew who had access to that room had the technical know how, the opportunity, or the gumption to create such an elaborate scheme. And there was no evidence that anything had been rigged that could have caused the effect.

A ghost seemed even less likely because, well, you know… ghosts probably don't exist. Not to mention that simply blaming a ghost risked giving short shrift to the possibility that Santa did it, elves did it, leprechauns did it (sprites, nymphs, fairies, banshees, etc.), and who's got time to disprove all of *that?*

This left number 3: I had dreamt the experience.

Wow! So *that's* what a hypnogogic experience is like. Hypnogogia is the state of consciousness when you're on your way to being fully asleep. It's a kind of gray zone where you have some sense of being aware and conscious, but you're also susceptible to dreamlike influences. This is not sleep paralysis, a state in which you can't move. In fact, this state might have the opposite effect and cause you to kick at something that isn't there. What's so convincing about a hypnogogic experience is that you might *think* you're awake, but you're not, at least not fully. That makes the dreamt element seem all the more real. And boy, did it feel real.

The hypnogogic experience has a sister: Hypnopompic experience. Having a hypnopompic experience is very similar to a hypnogogic occurrence in that the in-between (consciousness and wakefulness) aspect is the same. But in the hypnopompic experience, one is in the process of waking up, as opposed to falling asleep. But you're still not fully awake. Here's where sleep paralysis can get you because you could be in the middle of a REM phase and dreaming vividly.

But sleep paralysis is only one thing that can happen to you in a hypnogogic or hypnopompic state. You might see things that aren't there, hear things when there was no sound, or even feel something in the bed with you. As distressing as all these experiences can be, none are actually happening—at least outside of your own brain. The sights, sounds and physical contact you get from these states are all due to dream elements being conflated with consciousness. When you start stirring the awake pot into the asleep pot, all kinds of crazy things can happen.

When people come to me and tell me about their wacky ghost and paranormal stories (this happens a lot) the first thing I always ask is, "What time of day this this happen?"

The majority answer, "At night."

"Were you in bed?"

"Yes."

The "Were you asleep?" follow-up question is trickier. During the hypnogogic and hypnopompic states, that's not such an easy question to answer. It might *feel* like you're awake, but the ghoul at the end of your bed might suggest otherwise.

There are a couple of other strange experiences that a semi-conscious state can trigger—both of which I've gone through.

The first is missing time. Alien abduction stories (think of the Barney and Betty Hill case) sometimes have an element of lost time to them. For example, it's 1:00 a.m., and the next thing you know, it's 4:00 a.m. While driving through Oklahoma, that exact thing happened to me. I had already been driving for 10 or 12 hours on my way to Los Angeles from Chicago. After unsuccessfully trying to take a nap at a truck stop near Tulsa, I decided to keep driving. I remember looking at the dashboard clock when I got back on the road and seeing that it was a bit after 1:00 a.m. The next time I looked down—which seemed like only a few minutes later—it was 5:30 a.m., and I was already seeing road signs for Amarillo, Texas. The sky was already starting to grow light behind me. I had traveled over 300 miles in what seemed like an instant.

Did I pass through some Okie wormhole and pop out in the Lone Star State?

Probably not.

We can assume that I wasn't actually asleep the whole time because the truck would have drifted off the road. But it is conceivable that I was in some sort of deep thought or even a light hypnogogic twilight for quite some time. I was awake enough to sense traffic and keep the truck between the ditches, but asleep enough to make over 4 hours seem like only 4 minutes. We know that 8 hours of sleep doesn't *feel* like 8 hours, so it seems reasonable that a semi-conscious state might also speed the perception of time.

The other perception-warping thing that happened to me also involved driving late at night. I was on the road during a comedy tour through Wisconsin. Three hours into the drive, I was relaxed and lost in thought when I saw in the distance what looked like a brontosaurus. (It might have been a diplodocus or some other sauropod, but you get the picture.) When I first saw it, I smiled and thought to myself, "That's pretty cool." It was well in the distance, and backlit—I really only saw its silhouette—and it clearly had that long neck and the classic curves on its massive body.

It occurred to me that it might be an old Sinclair gas station. Some of them had big ol' brontosauruses next to the stations to draw attention. But as I got closer, it became evident that this thing was *much* bigger than a fiberglass model. My brontosaurus was frickin' *huge*—it was multiple stories high and must have weighed hundreds of tons! And it wasn't looking any less like a brontosaurus as I drew closer. My smile of appreciation turned to wonder—then awe. What IS that thing? It can't be a brontosaurus. Obviously! Yet there it was, getting bigger and bigger as I sped down this central Wisconsin highway. I laughed to myself, "This is unbelievable!"

Just as I got to the point where the massive beast would almost be looming over me... bam! The angle changed and the whole thing reformed itself into a rock formation and some trees. Ok, it didn't actually do anything. My *perception* of it shifted just enough to see it for what it really was—a commonplace chunk of roadside real estate.

So what caused this prehistoric beast to appear, then vanish? Two factors. First, I was in that same relaxed state while driving at night, and not focused on anything in particular. This allowed me to drift in and out of being aware of my surroundings. But what really opened the door for me to see a dinosaur in Wisconsin is something called pareidolia.

Pareidolia is when the brain perceives a pattern of something where that thing doesn't actually exist. We humans are pattern-seeking animals, and that tendency has served us well over the last 100,000 years. Being able to pick out potentially dangerous faces, shapes, and even sounds from the randomness of a landscape can be a life-extending skill. But that skill's switch may also be "on" in everyday situations when you really aren't in any danger from a brontosaurus or anything else. We regularly see faces and familiar shapes in random everyday scenery, but pareidolia tells you that you just drove your car into the Jurassic period.

My own experiences remind me that we can have convincingly wacky experiences and not be the least bit crazy. Our brains are more than capable of deceiving us, even if they are in perfect working order, and consulting other people and other methods, rather than relying solely on our often faulty senses, is the whole idea behind science.

And it can help determine if it's your own mind just pulling your leg.

James Underdown is the Executive Director of the Center for Inquiry-Los Angeles. He is also the founder of the Independent Investigations Group, an organization that investigates extraordinary claims and offers $100,000 to anyone who can prove paranormal or supernatural ability under test conditions. In the late 1970s, James wrestled Victor the Wrestling Bear, although nowadays he spends his time wrestling psychic mediums, such as Rebecca Rosen, John Edward and James Van Praagh. He has appeared on numerous TV shows, including the Discover Channel's "Weird or What?," the "Dr. Phil show," and Penn & Teller's "Bullshit!"

Escape From Alcatraz

Jeff Wagg

I believed in the supernatural.

It was the summer of 1996—the Fourth of July weekend. My then-wife (we're now divorced) and I were entertaining family in our new townhouse in Reston, Virginia. We were quite popular with our family because we had provided the first baby. His name was Fisher, and he had supernatural powers.

A baby with supernatural powers wasn't something I believed easily. Earlier that summer, I had read Carl Sagan's *The Demon Haunted World: Science as a Candle in the Dark.* I knew how we fool ourselves by misinterpreting what we see, often seeing only what we want. But I didn't want the kid to be supernatural. I only believed he was because of what happened.

As we entertained often, I bought a number of board games and kinetic puzzles to entertain visitors. Remember, 1996 was pre-smartphone—we actually had to rely on physical objects for amusement. One of these puzzles was a simple toy called "Alcatraz." It was a cage, with the base, top and two supports made of plastic, and four brass poles for bars. Inside the cage was a ball bearing the size of a 25¢ gumball. You know the kind. At least you would if you were as old as me.

Alcatraz: The Puzzle
(Photo: Infinite Innovations)

Removing the ball from its puny penitentiary seemed impossible. The solution didn't come with the toy, and you couldn't Google it because Google hadn't been invented yet. You had to mail a card to get the answer. I did this, but back in the days of snail mail it would take weeks to get a reply. That didn't matter. In the meantime I was determined to prove how clever I was, so I set to work trying to free the ball.

Some puzzles, like Rubik's Cube, offer many choices. You can spin the blocks various ways but not be sure if you're getting closer to the goal. With Alcatraz, there was nothing to spin. No buttons, or levers. No combination or locks to pick. The four brass poles spun a little, but nothing gave way, and applying pressure was useless. I know this because I pressed everywhere on the thing and nothing happened.

My wife and her sister, who was staying with us for the summer as a nanny, also had no luck in getting it open. Various aunts and uncles gave Alcatraz a try over the weekend, but the ball remained a prisoner. Could it be that the puzzle-maker was playing a trick on us? Probably not, but I was beginning to suspect that the solution involved something that wasn't included in the package.

As it turned out, that something was my seven-month-old son, Fisher.

We were playing dominoes on the coffee table. Fisher occasionally grabbed a domino before we could stop him, but we weren't too concerned about him swallowing it. Honestly, we were mostly worried about him ruining our game. (It's a parent thing—you gradually learn that you don't have to watch your kid every single second.) When he somehow grabbed Alcatraz, we remained unalarmed. So long as the ball was safely trapped in its cage, he could shake it and chew on it while we finished our game of dominoes.

We finished the game (I won!) and as tradition held, the losers had to reset the dominoes. While they were doing this, I looked over at Fisher. He was still busy with Alcatraz, except that the cage was empty and the ball was lying on the floor next to him! At this point, the ball was a hazard so I took it away while I examined the cage, slack-jawed. One of the poles was detached at one end and it swung away far enough to allow the ball to pass through.

I examined the cage and ball, baffled. Even with the ball free, I couldn't figure out how it worked. The pole refused to go back in place, and there were still no obvious catches or release mechanisms. Everyone gave it a try, although no one was able to put it back the way it was. Fisher wasn't too pleased with having his new toy taken away, so the nanny suggested that we give him the cage back without the ball. "Fine," I said.

We played another game of dominoes, but my head wasn't really in it. How had Fisher solved the puzzle? Did gumming the bars toothlessly do something that pressing on it hadn't? Was drool a factor? It didn't make sense. In the middle of the game, I glanced back at Fisher.

He had put the cage back together again.

I took it from him. Sure enough, the cage was securely locked, though the ball was safely in my pocket. I was dumbfounded. My best explanation was that the kid was some kind of prodigy puzzle solver. Consider the facts: Multiple adults had tried and failed to open this puzzle. And none of them could close the cage when it was opened either. In just minutes, Fisher had opened the puzzle *and* closed it again. And we're talking about a baby here, not even a toddler. He couldn't walk or even talk, much less plot some kind of trickery.

My wife suggested we see if Fisher could find a way to put the ball back in the cage. I didn't think he'd even understand the concept that the ball belonged in the cage, but I had another concern. As a child I'd swallowed a ball bearing, so I wasn't comfortable with him playing with the pieces. But she really wanted to try, and agreed to watch him closely. I went to look through the trash for the original packaging. I needed an answer, and thought it unlikely but possible that there was something written on the box that would offer a clue.

As I dug through papers, banana peels, and coffee grounds, I was overtaken by a sensation. It's how one might feel after finding a box containing a singing frog in an abandoned building.

My son was Michigan J. Frog, and I was special because he was mine. What else could he do? What amazing things did the future hold?

I wasn't able to find the package, but I was elated. I hurried back into the room to find everyone gathered in silence around my Fisher.

The ball was back in the cage.

The puzzle was sitting on the floor next to him, as if he'd lost interest in it, having solved it at least four times (open/close/open/close).

Perhaps we could find a Gordian knot for him to try?

I let out an exasperated "*What?*" and my wife and her sister the nanny giggled. And suddenly… all my belief came crashing down. It was obvious what had happened—one of them had solved the puzzle secretly, and then arranged things so it would look like Fisher was doing everything. I thought back and realized that I only saw the results of Fisher's amazing abilities and never the process of him actually solving the puzzle.

I accused them.

"Ok, so which one of you solved it?"

The nanny answered: "Neither of us figured it out. Fisher got the ball out on his own."

My wife nodded her head in agreement.

But at this point the jig was up. I believed her, but my wife's certainty that her sister was telling the truth also told me that she shared knowledge of what was really going on. I had another puzzle to solve.

"So you two know what's going on?"

"Yes. Fisher got the ball out of the cage."

They giggled a bit more.

"And he put it back by himself?"

"Well, no. He had a bit of help with that."

The nanny seemed to be enjoying this immensely.

"Ah, I see. So if you didn't figure out the puzzle, how did you know how to close it?"

"You did it. You provided the solution."

"I did?"

"Yes."

I took a moment to consider the situation. I hadn't solved the puzzle, and yet somehow I'd provided the solution to them. How could that be? And then I remembered that I had mailed away for the solution. But that didn't make sense: Even if it had arrived unusually fast, she wouldn't have opened my mail. Yet, it was all I had to go with.

"Wait, you didn't open my mail, did you?"

"No. I wouldn't do that."

So much for that. How the heck did *I* provide the solution?

She let me stew for a moment and then explained, "I didn't have to open your mail. They didn't send the answer in a letter."

I waited.

"It was a postcard."

I let out an exasperated scream, and laughed, not only at their well-played gag, but at my foolishness for believing that there was something supernatural going on. She showed me the card and then I knew the solution as well. We each took a turn removing the ball from the cage and placing it back. The puzzle was solved, and my son reverted back to simply being "super," rather than "supernatural."

But Fisher's aunt, the nanny, made a very astute observation. Now that we knew the solution, it was obvious that a baby would have an easier time solving the puzzle than an adult.

Why? Because babies will do things that adults won't.

And what that thing is, I leave for you to figure out.

Jeff Wagg went from believing in the power of spells and mind-over-matter to managing the Million Dollar Paranormal Challenge for legendary skeptic, James "The Amazing" Randi. Today, he curates the College of Curiosity, an organization dedicated to changing perspectives through field trips and other projects. He lives in Chicago with his wife and various animals. http://collegeofcuriosity.com

I Tawt I Taw A Puddy Tat!

David Waldron

Over the years, skeptics have developed the rather unflattering reputation of being closed-minded sticks in the mud who are devoid of imagination. For some, this reputation is not undeserved. As a folklorist, I have certainly seen my share of people who become contemptuous of anyone with an interest in folklore and mythological heritage. However, this is far from the norm. I believe that most skeptics, like myself, are fired by a deep and abiding sense of curiosity and a desire to explore what lies behind the stories people tell about their experiences of "high strangeness."

Far from a dry desire to take away people's stories or to mess with their imaginative play, I love storytelling, mythology and culture. I find stories of high strangeness to be insightful, moving, creative, and filled with wonder, and I enjoy the prickle up the spine created by a well-told ghost story on a dark evening. I adore fantasy and science fiction literature and I find the connection between place, heritage, and culture to be deeply profound. I confess to having a love of Neolithic ruins in the British Isles and spent time enjoying the atmosphere in the Cairns of Camster, Cuwen's Tomb, and the many stone circles that dot the British Isles. When I was writing *Sign of the Witch: Modernity and the Pagan Revival*, I delighted in attending a Pagan festival, enjoying the spectacle of the ritual and the warmth of spiced mead and roasted lamb on a cold winter's night. I can enjoy stories of high strangeness as stories but not feel the need for them to be "real" to appreciate them and the lessons contained within.

At the same time, it is important to be introspective about these stories. What do they really mean? Why do we find them so emotionally powerful? What do they tell us about who we are and where we have come from? In the modern world, we experience that sense of duality between a heritage of rich folklore and culture that is tempered by an education defined by the enlightenment tradition of reason, logic, and science. And so, we all have those moments where we put reason aside to feel the enormous emotional power of a shared mythology and culture; even if only by being creeped out by a good monster story.

So, let's move on to my own monster story.

One of Australia's most pervasive legends is that large cat-like predators roam the bush. Big cats are not native to Australia, so how did they supposedly arrive there? The most popular theory claims that during World War II, American servicemen smuggled pumas or black panthers into Australia as military mascots but then abandoned them in the bush before leaving the country. Now, the descendants of these creatures wander the landscape preying on sheep, cattle, and native wildlife.

This legend has been reinforced by numerous unconfirmed sightings of mysterious big cats all over the country, particularly in the Blue Mountains area near Sydney. The legend is so woven into local lore that their rugby league football team is named the Penrith Panthers. Reports of big cats are also common in the Gippsland region of Victoria. In fact, the stories are so persistent that in 2012, the Victorian government was pressured to engage in an official study of the possible existence of big cats. I was fortunate to be heavily involved in this project due to my work on this subject in *Snarls from the Tea-tree: Victoria's Big Cat Folklore.* The study concluded that there wasn't any sound evidence for big cats in the region and suggested that people were seeing large feral domestic cats instead.

But this hasn't silenced the legend.

Growing up around the town of Warragul, Gippsland, I remember the urban legends well. I was a member of the Boy Scouts, and we told stories of big cats around the campfire. During car trips I stared out the window hoping to catch a glimpse of a big cat. When there was a spate of livestock killings, big cats would be blamed. Funnily enough, when I began researching the subject as an adult I found that, far from being a modern story tied to U.S. servicemen, the legend was already present from the time of colonization. Every time the story re-emerged, a new origin myth developed. Over the past 200 years, stories of mystery marsupial cats that escaped from circuses or private menageries and tales of giant cats released by Chinese immigrants on the goldfields were all variations of the very same legend.

There was a lot more to this story than a simple belief that big cats were released into the Australian bush. The legend was an expression of what novelist Marcus Clarke described as the "Australian Gothic"—the experience of immigrants coming to terms with an alien and harsh landscape. There was the expectation of finding the exotic animals that inhabit our neighboring Asian countries. The legend was also tied to the disaster of the acclimatization societies—organizations that introduced rabbits, rats, mice and other invasive flora and fauna into Australia, with disastrous results. This led to enormous anxiety in the newspapers, in which people feared big cats escaping from a traveling circus or private collection, or that deadly animals might turn feral in the same way that escaped or released rabbits and pigs had. These fears were tied to poor farming practices that caused a loss of livestock, and damage wrought by tree removal that forced dingoes and feral dogs onto farmland to forage for food. The legend was also linked to anti-American sentiment after a ruling in 1942 that Australian troops overseas were not allowed to keep mascots, for fear they would bring diseased or dangerous animals back into the country, while American troops on Australian soil were allowed to keep their mascots.

So, the tales of big cats that I grew up with were already well entrenched in our culture. These stories had a sense of plausibility about them and were inextricably tied to a wide array of social and cultural issues.

It was within this context that I saw my monster.

Several years before I began my big cat research—indeed this incident inspired my work—I was driving to my parent's home in Ballarat. It was approximately 2 a.m., and I was passing around a bend near the rural town of Anakie where, to my astonishment, I saw a large cat-like animal on the road ahead of me. It was crouched low with its flexible tail sticking up in the air, shaped like an inverted "J." The animal was pitch-black in color and I saw a flash of bright yellow from its eyes. It was so large that it seemed to stretch across the entire width of the road. The creature looked up at me as I slowly approached and then with a few quick bounds it disappeared into the bush across the other side of the road.

The experience was startling. It was the very kind of thing I had hoped for when I was a young boy camping late at night, looking for a sense of wonder and mystery in the prosaic world. What was also peculiar is that, despite my shock and immense curiosity, I did not stop to take a closer look. Perhaps because it was late at night and I was exhausted. But I also felt that sense of high strangeness, even fear, and so I didn't investigate the matter further. I had the feeling that I was tapping into much older, primal sensations of anxiety surrounding the legacy of predators and being aware of prey. I recall a friend of mine telling me he had experienced this during a hiking trip in northern Australia when he heard large crocodiles moving along a nearby river bank at night. It was a feeling with which we are unfamiliar today: The knowledge that we have predators and we are on the menu. In that time of night we are also prone to hypnogogic states and the play of imagination, and these kinds of feelings loom much larger than in the light of day. This is much like those nights when, as a child, you sit in your bedroom, forming shapes out of the darkness.

So, I continued driving, feeling puzzled all the way home.

But let's think about it for a moment. What did I really see? For just a few seconds, I saw a black shape on the road, with a flash of yellow eye reflection. Did I actually see a big cat, or did I see what folklore, combined with the effects of pareidolia and a lack of sleep, suggested to me out of the shadows? I saw the creature from a distance and in reviewing the literature of big cat sightings I am aware of the problems of judging scale, especially late at night. I had a personal experience but I cannot be certain that I saw what I thought I had seen, especially when my imagination was shaped by two centuries of cultural expectations entrenched in me since childhood. The more likely possibility was that I had seen a large feral cat, a dog from a certain angle, or a black rock wallaby.

Big Cat or Feral Cat?
(Photo: David Waldron)

I recall having a similar experience when I was researching the Black Dog of Bungay, or Black Shuck, as he is popularly called. I was back home in Australia when I heard a horrific scream coming from my neighbor's yard at 2 a.m. Still in my pajamas, I rushed outside to see our pet cat being attacked by what looked like an enormous black dog. I filled a bucket with water as a makeshift weapon but by the time I had arrived in the neighbor's yard my cat was already dead. Then the dog started to approach me, growling and snarling. He seemed sinister and of enormously muscular proportions. His head was like that of a crocodile—it was huge and triangular. Walking backwards with my pitiful bucket of water I retreated to my home and shut the gate. The next morning, I found the dog still in the neighbor's yard. In the light of day he looked like a perfectly normal pit bull mix. He was dark brown in color, not black, and only knee high, wagging his tail like nothing was ever the matter. The explanation was that the owner's house had been broken into and the dog had escaped in a state of panic, only to find himself stuck in the neighbor's backyard. I had even seen the dog before but had not made the association late at night when I was high on adrenaline.

During my research, a local big cat hunter took me out into the bush at night to listen for big cats. With a directional microphone in hand, we spent hours in pitch darkness listening to ambivalent sounds, waiting to hear something that sounds like a big cat. I quickly learned that people are unable to identity even ordinary sounds, such as the scream of a red fox, when they are emotionally entangled in the moment. One man showed me footage of a big cat and its cub only to see in the cold light of day that it was just an ordinary feral cat and its kitten. He was so perplexed that he thought someone must have tampered with his phone. Another hunter took me out to see many sheep kills where we found some black, foul-smelling goo on a leaf. He was certain it was a fur ball from a puma. I dutifully took the goo to my University science department for analysis, which revealed the material to be desiccated frog eggs deposited by recent floods.

"Puma Fur Ball" (Desiccated Frog Eggs)
(Photo: David Waldron)

This pattern of shaping ordinary occurrences into ones of wonder and mystery became the staple of my time studying the folklore surrounding big cat stories. People's emotions would be quite genuine, and the reverence with which they would hold onto these signs of wonder and mystery was extraordinary. I came to see these experiences as a gestalt, where a wide array of disconnected phenomena, each element trivial on its own, would be woven together to create mysterious and magical experiences for people. They were a re-enchantment of the wilderness and a sense of feeling connected to something beyond the normal humdrum of daily life. Yet the emotions were real for the people who experienced them.

People should not be ridiculed for having strange experiences. In my case, the experience of seeing a "big cat" inspired me to research the phenomenon thoroughly and critically, but with an eye to understanding what the stories mean to those who tell them.

Dr. David Waldron is a lecturer in History and Anthropology at Federation University in Ballarat, Australia, with a research focus on folklore and community identity. He has a Ph.D. in history from the University of Ballarat. David is the author of *Sign of the Witch: Modernity and the Pagan Revival; Shock! The Black Dog of Bungay: a Case Study in Local Folklore; Snarls from the Tea-Tree: Victoria's Big Cat Folklore,* and *The Goldfields and the Gothic: A Hidden Heritage and Folklore.*

A (Big) Foot In The Door

Anonymous

I have a story to tell.

It was a Saturday morning and my friend Chris and I wondered what we would do that night.

"Why don't we go to the cabin?" I suggested.

My uncle Peter owned a cabin in Inverness, California, a little community near the Point Reyes shoreline. "Cabin" makes it sound like some sort of quaint lodge or romantic hideaway, but it was just a rundown old shack. He refused to keep a television or any other modern conveniences. It didn't even have heat—but at least I had the keys to the place. Well, I knew that he kept a spare key under the proverbial doormat. My uncle rarely visited the cabin, so we often did.

We also invited our friend, Tim, but his parents were forcing him to attend his cousin's wedding. He said he might join us later on, if he could skip out on the reception.

That afternoon Chris and I hit the road, singing along with the Red Hot Chili Peppers. We stopped at a grocery store in the hippie town of Fairfax to load up on junk food. To our complete disappointment, the place turned out to be a health food store. We soon emerged with the unhealthiest things we could find—yogurt-covered raisins, some carob candy bars, and a bag of lentil chips.

With that lineup of awful snacks the nightmare had begun; little did we know there was worse to come.

After getting lost on the winding roads in Inverness, we finally arrived at the cabin. We grabbed our stuff out of the car and headed up the path to the door. But this time I didn't even have to search for the key under the doormat: The door was already open.

The Cabin
(Photo: The Author)

I crept inside and walked around quietly in case the intruder was still there. The cabin was empty. From the looks of the place, someone had broken in looking for something to steal but they had found only dusty, old furniture and lots of board games—my uncle's substitute for television. The angry burglar had overturned a chair, knocked down a table lamp and scattered a box of Trivial Pursuit cards across the floor. I would have called the cops about the break-in but nothing had been stolen and technically, we were trespassing too.

We cleaned up the place a bit and did what any youths would do in our situation: We raided the pantry. But all we could find was some Dinty Moore beef stew, baked beans, sardines and a few packets of hot cocoa that had expired a few months before.

"Don't worry," Chris said brightly. "If we mix it all together it'll taste all right."

We sat down at the kitchen table with our carob bars and cups of warm cocoa to play a game of Trivial Pursuit. One of the questions was about the classic Bigfoot movie, *The Legend of Boggy Creek*. This incited a passionate argument about which Bigfoot movie was the best of all time. We both believed in Bigfoot in those days. We lived near Bigfoot country and had heard and seen weird things during camping trips. Besides, we'd watched that Patterson-Gimlin film—it was clear proof of the existence of Bigfoot.

Before cracking open the can of Dinty Moore beef stew for dinner, we decided to take a walk through the woods to find some branches to build a fire. Most of the trees were covered in a rich, green moss, and it was the rainy season, so it was difficult to find any dry wood. With patience, we slowly started to amass a pile of twigs, branches, and small logs. By then it was starting to get dark and I thought it was time to get back to the cabin.

Suddenly, I smelled a foul stench in the air. It reeked like a dead, rotting animal. Chris crinkled his nose and looked at me—he'd smelled it too.

"Phew!" he said in disgust. "It smells like something died out here."

"Thought you'd just opened that can of Dinty Moore stew," I joked.

Then I had the feeling that we were being watched. I looked around but I couldn't see anyone. The nearest neighbors were over a mile away.

We were standing still when we heard a twig snap.

"What was that?" Chris asked.

"I dunno," I replied with a frown. "Maybe there's a skunk around."

Then we heard the snapping sound again. And again. We started hearing strange noises all around us and they seemed to be getting closer.

Chris pointed ahead. "What the fuck is that?" he asked.

I looked up and saw a tall, dark shape standing behind a tree about 30 feet away from us.

"Hey!" I yelled at it bravely and stupidly. "Who's there?"

But there was no reply.

As we stared at the shape it seemed to blend into the background until it disappeared.

Then we both heard a deep growl right next to us.

"Shit! Shit! Shit!" we screamed as we hightailed it back to the cabin, leaving behind our stash of firewood.

The Woods
(Photo: The Author)

We reached the cabin and ran inside. I slammed the door and locked it tight. We pulled the drapes across the windows and stood in the kitchen, trying to catch our breath. We both wanted to look outside to see what it was, but we didn't want *it* to see *us*.

What had we just seen and heard? The grunt-like growl sounded like a fierce animal of some kind. Whatever it was, it definitely wasn't human.

We sat down on the kitchen floor, listening carefully. But everything had gone quiet.

All of a sudden we heard a thud above us. It sounded like a rock had been thrown at the roof. It rolled down the tiles and dropped onto the ground. Then we heard another rock hitting the roof. And another. And another. It sounded like rocks were raining down from the sky.

Bad smells, strange noises, grunts and growls, and a hail of rocks. From reading books and watching movies I knew that these were obvious signs of Bigfoot activity.

"I think it's Bigfoot," Chris said, reading my mind.

We sat there in silence for the longest time.

Just as it seemed as though the threat had passed and we began to calm down, the front doorknob started to turn. But the door wouldn't open because we had locked it. The doorknob rattled violently. Soon the entire door shook from the force of this "thing" trying to break into the cabin to get to us.

Then it stopped. We held our breath. It seemed like we sat there, huddled together on the floor, for an hour or more. But it was probably only five minutes. Had the creature given up? We had a whisper argument over who was going to check to see what was out there.

Chris lost.

He made his way to the door slowly, dragging his feet all the way. He unlocked it noiselessly and peered out timidly through the opening.

"Aaarrrggghhh!" cried the beast.

A foot wedged its way in the door and pried it open, slamming it against the wall.

The "beast" was Tim.

"You fucking douche bag!" I cried. "You scared the shit out of us!"

"Well then, mission accomplished," Tim said with an evil laugh.

He'd attended his cousin's wedding and then skipped the reception to make his way out to Inverness to hang out with us. We were pissed at him for his prank, but he had brought beef jerky, a bag of Doritos, and some beer, so we let him stay.

Later that night, after a dinner of Dinty Moore beef stew, we were sitting around, drinking beer and already laughing about the events of the day.

"You should've seen the look on your faces when I busted open the door!" said Tim.

"We were freaked out," I admitted. "By then you'd been terrorizing us for hours."

"It was creepy when you were standing behind that tree," said Chris. "And even creepier when you suddenly appeared right next to us and growled."

"And you scared the crap out of us when you threw all of those rocks on the roof," I added.

Tim frowned.

"What do you mean?" he said with sincerity. "I didn't do *any* of that."

We all stared at each other in shock.

Over the years, I've wondered who or what terrorized Chris and me that day. Perhaps it was a homeless person who was squatting in the empty cabin. Maybe it was a black bear that had previously broken in and returned looking for food. Or it's possible that we'd just heard ordinary animal sounds in the woods and the dark shape we saw behind the tree was pareidolia.

But I'm going to say we encountered Bigfoot that day because I have a story to tell.

For the past 20 years, Anonymous has written for various science-based publications. He lives in the San Francisco Bay Area with two cats and a guinea pig. As far as he knows, he is no relation to the Anonymous who over millennia has been credited with authoring numerous aphorisms, songs, plays, and short stories.

Bear In Mind:

Afterword
James E. Alcock

Have you seen any leprechauns lately? Maybe a mermaid while out to sea? Or a fairy at the end of your garden?

Probably not. And even if you have, no one will believe you; your account will only elicit snickers. Yet, people took reports of such sightings very seriously in years gone by.

But suppose that you tell of a ghost or a UFO. Or a vivid dream that foretold a traumatic event. No snickers this time. Instead, people perk up their ears and ask for details. Yet, there is no reliable evidence that such phenomena are any more real than leprechauns, mermaids or fairies. And in fact, there is plenty of good reason to believe that they are just as imaginary.

Nonetheless, this book has demonstrated that just about everyone has had an experience that seems to defy logic and call for a paranormal explanation, and some people have such experiences on a regular basis. What is going on?

Given the complexity of our brains, it would be surprising if we did *not* have strange experiences from time to time, even if nothing paranormal is going on. To understand how this is so, it's important to consider how our experiences are formed in general.

Our "consciousness," with which we examine, contemplate, apply logic (sometimes!) and draw conclusions, is only part of a very complex information-processing system. Our brains are constantly processing vast amounts of information, quickly, automatically and without conscious awareness. These conscious and non-conscious systems generally work well together, and as a result, well-learned behaviors—such as driving a car, brushing your teeth, or walking upstairs without tripping—can be accomplished on "auto pilot" without conscious intervention.

However, there are times when non-conscious processing unexpectedly pops into consciousness and provides us with information that is astonishing, because we have no idea where it came from. Say you visit your Uncle Harry, and although you are not explicitly aware of it, the non-conscious part of your brain notes that he is moving a bit more slowly than usual, that he smiles less often, and that he did not have his usual second cup of coffee. You leave without any thoughts of Uncle Harry ailing, but some signs of that have registered non-consciously. Later that night, these hints are manifested in a nightmare in which Uncle Harry dies. In the morning you shake off the dream as meaningless, but when Uncle Harry drops dead two days later, you are shocked not only by his death but by the recollection of your "psychic" dream.

Did you predict the future? Well, not really. Instead, the non-conscious part of your brain was aware of danger signals although the conscious part was not.

A number of other ways our brains work are also important for understanding how we can have experiences that seem to defy normal explanation.

Agency Detection

It is difficult to shrug off what seems to have been a psychic dream as a meaningless "trick of the night." When no explanation is obvious, this prompts many people to consider the experience paranormal. Why are we so keen to find explanations? It is built right into us. Our brains are set up to seek causes for the events around us: That is, to detect *agency*. This is important for our survival. By the time children are only a year old, they are already beginning to interpret events as having been *caused* by something, by some sort of agent. A ball does not roll into view on its own; somebody or something caused it to move. And so, as adults, we automatically interpret events in terms of agency, even when we cannot see the agents. You hear a loud noise in the sky; without looking up, you know there is an airplane above. You hear that barking sound? A dog is nearby. You see a flash of light on your living room wall at night—your curtains are open, and a car's headlights just illuminated your room. You suddenly feel cold—it is wintertime and somebody opened the door.

But what happens when our agency detection fails to find an agent? You are sitting in your living room and a ball suddenly rolls in front of you—but you are alone in the house. There is a flash of light on your living room wall—but your curtains are closed. Or you suddenly feel the room grow cold while alone at night in an old, creaky house. Because you don't detect an agent immediately, your nervous system reacts with anxiety. When a natural explanation is not obvious, it is tempting to believe that something supernatural has occurred.

Expectation

The type of supernatural explanation will depend upon the socio-cultural context in which a person grew up, as shaped by the beliefs expressed by parents and teachers and friends and neighbors. Roman Catholics may encounter the Virgin Mary, but Hindus never do. Haitians may experience the power of Voodoo, while those unfamiliar with such magic are immune. And we all may experience what seems to be telepathy, or a ghost, because such interpretations fit in with widely held beliefs.

Reality Testing

As we grow up, we are taught to distinguish reality from fantasy. Children awakened by a nightmare are assured by their parents that bad dreams are "not real." By adulthood, we all accept that fairies, the Easter Bunny, or a Genie in a bottle—things that we have never actually seen—are fantasy, while other things we have never seen— viruses, atoms, and black holes—are real.

But when a situation is accompanied by strong emotions, reality testing can break down, leaving us vulnerable to mistaking the unreal for the real. For example, one night a friend of mine had an upsetting dream—he described it as being much more vivid and "real" than a normal dream—involving the funeral of his favorite uncle. He was shaken by the dream and said that even though he did not believe in precognition, he feared that if his uncle died in the near future, he would be unable to resist feeling that something paranormal had occurred. He recognized and even feared the power of emotion over reason. However, when his uncle was still alive years later, reason won out.

Psychologist Ray Hyman has regularly warned that no one, skeptics included, should consider themselves immune to the effects of powerful emotional experiences that cry out for paranormal explanation.

But there is even more to consider in terms of how our brains leave us vulnerable to belief in the paranormal.

Perception

We never directly experience reality. Our brains automatically construct a model of the world that we take to be real. And most of the time, that model works very well. But that process of creating a model of reality is sometimes vulnerable to significant error. This is in part because of the power of the brain, not to its weakness. We are able to reach meaningful conclusions about reality based on incomplete information. If you *see* the hood of an Aston Martin peeking out from an alleyway, you *perceive* an automobile partially hidden from sight. You don't need to ask whether the rest of the car is actually there. If you *hear* a particular sound in the cloud-covered sky, you *perceive* that an airplane is passing overhead. Moreover, perception is influenced both by agency detection and expectation. If you see a shadowy movement in the bushes in your garden, your brain will fit that movement to the various templates it has available. As a result, you're unlikely to mistake the object for a gorilla if you have no reason to expect there is a gorilla in your neighborhood.

Memory

Just as perception is a constructive process, so too is memory. Each time an experience is brought to mind, that recollection is influenced not just by the original interpretation of the event, but by factors including subsequent information that one has obtained, one's mental and emotional state at the time of the recollection, and even the questions or events that trigger the recollection. A great deal of research has revealed how malleable our memories are and how little correspondence there often is between confidence in a memory and its accuracy. And each time we recollect an event, we unconsciously shape it in such a way as to make it more consistent with our interpretation of the event. As a result, reports of extraordinary experiences, even when held with high confidence, have proven to be very unreliable. And if you have had a "paranormal" experience, all you now have is your *memory* of it.

Temporal Contiguity

Our brains form associations between events that occur closely together in time. This is called temporal contiguity and it occurs automatically; we can't help ourselves. While this normally serves us well, it also leaves us open to being misled by the co-occurrence of two unrelated events. Because of this, we can easily develop personal superstitions, and we're shaken by powerful coincidences. Say you dream of an earthquake and the next day there is an earthquake; it is difficult to resist the belief that the two events are connected. (This again relates to agency detection.)

And while we remember the important coincidences, our memories are selective. You may have a dream that seemed to foretell an event, but when that event did not follow the dream, the dream is forgotten. But when the dream is followed by a corresponding event, then that pairing is likely to be remembered forever. If we were able to remember all the failed instances, we'd be less impressed by the memory of what seemed to be psychic.

Altered States of Consciousness

As we have seen in this book, there are various situations in which our ability to reality-test breaks down. Hallucinations, for example, are experiences that seem to be completely real even though they are not. Our brains are can produce very realistic although completely false perceptions of seeing or hearing a deceased person, of being outside our bodies, or of being drawn down a tunnel towards a bright light (the near-death experience). When such experiences occur, it is extremely difficult to consider them to be anything other than real.

We have also read a few stories about hypnogogic and hypnopompic sleep, the stages of sleep in which the conscious part of the brain interprets a blend of information coming both through the senses and from inside the brain itself to create an actual perception of the outside world. Reports of ghosts are common in such states. Related to this is sleep paralysis, a relatively common phenomenon in which people, although fast asleep, feel wide-awake. They experience terror because they also feel paralyzed and in the presence of threatening forces, such as demons or aliens. And because they are asleep, reality-testing does not occur.

Conclusion

These factors leave us all susceptible to confusing the unreal with the real.

As we try to make sense of mysterious and sometimes overwhelming experiences, we are at a great disadvantage because we are restricted only to the information available to the conscious part of our brain. This often tempts us to seek agency outside ourselves, in paranormal or religious forms. For some people, such explanations fit within their belief system; for others, they are jarringly at odds.

Hopefully the stories in this book, related by some very sensible people among us, have helped show that being rational is not always easy. And sometimes, being rational isn't as comforting, self-affirming, or even as fun, as the alternative. But maybe, in the end, it can help us to appreciate more of the mysteries of our world, and of our brains, in ways we had never imagined.

Would you believe it?

Dr. James Alcock is a Professor of Psychology at York University, where he has been on faculty since 1973. He has a longstanding interest in both the critical application of science to psychology and the psychology of belief, particularly those beliefs involving anomalous experiences. James is the author of *Parapsychology: Science or magic?* and *Science and Supernature*, and he is co-author of *A textbook of social psychology* and an *Introduction to Social Psychology: Global Perspectives*. He is co-editor of *Psi Wars* and the author of numerous book chapters, articles and papers, most of which deal with the psychology of belief.

About the Author

Karen Stollznow is the author of the novel *Hits & Mrs.,* and the non-fiction books *God Bless America, Language Myths, Mysteries and Magic,* and *Haunting America.* A co-host of the popular Monster Talk podcast, she has spent many years investigating psychics, ghosts, Bigfoot and other anomalous claims. A Doctor of Linguistics, she has taught at several universities in the United States and Australia, and was a Researcher at the University of California, Berkeley. Karen was born in Sydney, Australia, and she currently lives in Denver, Colorado, with her husband Matthew and their son Blade.

www.karenstollznow.com

Made in the USA
Lexington, KY
19 February 2017